Character Matters!

Raising Kids with
Values That Last

JOHN & SUSAN YATES

Baker Books

A Division of Baker Book House Co
Grand Rapids, Michigan 49516

Published by Baker Books
a division of Baker Book House Company
P.O. Box 6287, Grand Rapids, MI 49516-6287

New paperback edition published 2002

Previously published in by Word Publishing under the title *What Really Matters at Home: Eight Crucial Elements for Building Character in Your Family*

Printed in the United States of America

Library of Congress Cataloging–in–Publication Data is on file at the Library of Congress, Washington, D.C.

ISBN 0-8010-6410-4

Scripture is taken from the NEW AMERICAN STANDARD BIBLE. Copyright © The Lockman Foundation 1960, 1962, 1963, 1968, 1971, 1972, 1973, 1975, 1977. Used by permission.

For current information about all releases from Baker Book House, visit our web site:
http://www.bakerbooks.com

With grateful hearts to
our parents,

FRANCES ALLISON ALEXANDER
SYDENHAM B. ALEXANDER
SUE TUCKER YATES
F. OGBURN YATES, SR.,

who have demonstrated to us
and to countless others
maturity, wisdom, and character

CONTENTS

ACKNOWLEDGMENTS
(John and Susan)

*F*irst and foremost we are grateful to our parents, Fran and Syd Alexander, Sue Tucker Yates and F. Ogburn Yates, Sr., who courageously undertook the jobs of raising us! Most of the good things that we have learned about character come from them.

Our children, Allison, John, Christopher, Susy, and Libby, continue to teach us much about character. They are our greatest treasures and our dearest friends.

Ann Hibbard, our editor, close friend, and partner in ministry, encouraged us throughout the entire book and held us to a high standard. Special thanks to her husband Jim and children, Laura and Mark, who generously shared their mom.

We are grateful to John Viccellio, our good friend and garden enthusiast, for his help with the final chapter. Suzie Hancock and Linda Yarr gave us invaluable help with the manuscript. Frank and Joan Alexander, Fran and Catlin Cade, Syd and Laurie Alexander, and Elaine Metcalf provided helpful feedback on the content.

Many others helped along the way, especially Beth Spring, Tom Barratt, Elizabeth Said, and Ann and Doug Holladay. Mike and Gail Hyatt and Robert and Bobbie Wolgemuth were a real support in the publication of the first edition of this book. We are thankful to be a part of the wonderful publishing team at Baker Book House.

We are especially grateful to the people of the Falls Church (Episcopal). They are our "family," and their prayers and love support us in so many ways. We are privileged to continue to grow in character with them.

INTRODUCTION
(Susan)

*R*ecently two entirely different events in my life have caused me to ponder issues that I don't ordinarily focus on in my hectic daily schedule.

Allison, the eldest of our five children, is preparing to go off to college in just two weeks. Her leaving causes a wave of different emotions within my heart as John and I begin this new season of watching our children leave. There is pride in her—in who she is. I marvel at the lady she has become. There is a sense in which I know that I have watched God's grace at work in the raising of this precious daughter, for His grace has covered many of our parental blunders. Her faith is strong, and she has a quiet beauty that radiates self-confidence and security. There is also a sadness within my heart—the sadness of seeing not only my daughter but also my close friend move away. How I will miss her companionship.

Beneath the surface of so many jumbled emotions, several questions keep coming to mind. As I visualize her on campus, different scenarios appear: challenging classes, new friendships, parties, diverse life-styles. There will be the witty, attractive secularist in the classroom. Will she be discerning or taken in by the allure of intellectual elitism? She will be exposed to well-thought-out skepticism. Will it shake her or challenge her to reexamine her faith and grow stronger, wiser, and better grounded? Students around her will be indulging sexual desires. Will she be strong enough to resist temptation? The abundance of good activities will provide her with numerous opportunities to overcommit herself. Will she make wise decisions in how to spend her time? When she fails, will she have the wisdom to recognize failure and learn from her mistakes without succumbing to self-condemnation?

Beneath the different scenes are the underlying questions: *Is she equipped to go out on her own? Has she developed the character that will enable her to face and stand firm in whatever comes her way in life?*

The second event that has caused me to ponder deep questions has been the illness of a dear friend. Just this past week we found out that our close friend and partner on our church staff has Lou Gehrig's disease. He is only forty-one with a wife and three young children. A man of deep faith, he gave up a secure position several years ago to come to Washington, D.C., to minister to the street people. When the diagnosis was confirmed, John and I wept together with Logan and his wife MaryLyman. Whenever we think about the children and MaryLyman, we cry again. Yet God has been very present in the midst of all of this. Logan has said that God is in this and that his only desire is that God be honored through his illness.

Seeing a dear friend battle terminal illness causes me to wonder about my own maturity. It causes me to examine my own faith. And it raises several questions. Do I have what it takes to trust God to the end? Have I the strength of character to resist despair and hopelessness? When life does not go the way I want it to, do I question God's caring power or do I stand firm, trusting in His love? When I am tempted to stray, do I resist my natural desires and instead obey God? Do I acknowledge my failures and seek forgiveness? Do I have the strength of character that will equip me with a quiet confidence to stand firm in life's blessings and in life's challenges?

As I help Allison pack to leave, and as I watch Logan prepare to die, I ask the question: What *is* really important in life?

It is not education, accomplishments, material possessions, health, or significance.

It is *character* that will sustain a child, an adult, a family. As parents we want to raise confident children with a sense of destiny—kids who know who they are and where they are going. We want this for ourselves as well. Character isn't something we get and then just pass on to our children. All of our lives we, too, are growing; we never finish.

Developing a character that stands firm is not something that will happen automatically. Good character development is not a hit-or-miss process. We need goals for character development, and we need practical ways of achieving these goals. This is the reason for this book.

Our job as parents is to equip our children for life. Training in character development is the heart and soul of this task. A Christian home is not a perfect home. Instead, it is a place where people are continually in process, a place where parents and children are growing.

This book is not a psychological analysis of character development. It is not a book of crafts to help teach our children character. It is not a book of specific activities that help teach character. It is not a description of how to build character into our children alone.

It is not education, accomplishments, material possessions, health, or significance. It is character that will sustain a child, an adult, a family.

It is a book describing how parents and children and singles can grow in character through the normal, daily events in our lives. This book highlights eight essential character traits and our understanding of God's perspective on each. Through numerous stories and many practical examples, we share how we are seeking to develop these traits in our own lives and in the lives of our children. By seeing how to use everyday circumstances as opportunities for character development, we realize that often the big lessons in life are best learned in the little, everyday issues.

We are not parents who have successfully raised five children of impeccable character. Our sixteen-year-old still rolls his eyes with that exasperated expression that seems to say, "If only my parents were as mature as I am," when reminded again to do what we have asked. Our eleven-year-old daughters still fuss with their fourteen-year-old brother.

Neither are we adults of sterling character. I continue to say things to my husband that I regret within five minutes.

Indeed in a home with kids eighteen, sixteen, fourteen, and twins nearly twelve and two strong-willed, opinionated parents, we are in the school of character building. We are not parents who have finished, rather we are people in process. We have learned that there is a great freedom and a great joy in growing in character together. This process is what this book is all about.

ва   ва   ва

Writing a book with your mate is a great and wonderful challenge. It has forced us to clarify what we believe and how we feel about many things. After much initial experimentation, we concluded that we could write this book most effectively if we each wrote different chapters on our own. And so each chapter is primarily the written work of one or the other of us and is written in the voice of that primary author. However, we have shared totally in determining the contents of every chapter. We are in complete agreement on each principle. In this endeavor we have become even more convinced that husbands and wives can work together as a team, complementing each other's individual perspectives. In this whole process, we have learned from each other and helped each other grow. We are grateful for all that it has done for us and pray that these chapters will be especially helpful and encouraging to you.

THE CRISIS OF CHARACTER
(John)

ONE

Sow a thought, reap an action; sow an action, reap a habit; sow a habit, reap a character; sow a character, reap a destiny.

UNKNOWN

The following true stories put into perspective some fundamental issues involved in becoming people of mature character. They illustrate two popular philosophies which have led us into a contemporary crisis of character.

Eight-year-old Lenore had not straightened her room when her mom told her. In fact, the room was in shambles and looked like a tornado had whipped through. Lenore had disregarded her mother's instructions and was about to run off to play with her best friend.

"Lenore," her mom called, "I told you that your room had to be straightened before you left. You knew this and you had plenty of time to clean it up, but you haven't done it. I'm sorry but I cannot let you go over to Betty's house. You will have to stay home and clean your room."

"But Mom," Lenore wailed, "you know how much this means to me. *Don't you want me to be happy?*"

To this her mother replied, "Of course I want you to be happy. I love you very much. But making sure that you are always having fun is not my goal. I'm trying to help you grow up to be a responsible, good young lady."

Fortunately, this wise mother had a clear sense of her goal for her daughter, but another true story gives a very different perspective.

A talented man became a success in his profession. Awards for his professional accomplishments accumulated, and material benefits enabled his family to have the best. However, he is a self-centered person and talks only about subjects which are of interest to him. He seems to have no concept of serving others, yet he is unaware of this lack in himself. He is a difficult person to like and difficult for his family to live with.

What responsibility do his parents have for his egotistical personality? Who can say? Yet a small anecdote from his childhood is rather telling. One evening years ago when he was a teenager, he and his mother were watching the evening news. Listening to the reports of escalating warfare, a war in which many American soldiers were involved, he fearfully asked his mother, "Mom, will I ever have to go to war? Will I ever have to fight?"

His mother hugged him and reassured him, then she promised him that she would make sure he would never have to be a soldier.

Not many parents would want their children to have to go to war, and none of us would disagree with this parent's desire to comfort her child. Yet she was wrong not only to make such a promise but also to miss the opportunity to talk with her son about trust in God, self-sacrifice, love, and doing for others. If this young man was indeed raised on the philosophy that "Mom will keep you from all difficult situations and unhappiness," he was indeed done a great disservice.

A subtle yet dangerous message is illustrated by both of these stories, a message that says, *"Your happiness is the most important thing in the world."* Our job as parents is not to make our children happy. Naturally, we want happiness for our children, but this cannot be our primary goal, because the result will be an unhappy self-centered person.

Some time ago Bobby McFerrin made popular a song with the refrain, "Don't worry, Be happy." How nice it would be if life were so simple. But it is not, and when happiness is our goal, disappointment will result.

Many a parent has been made to feel guilty by a manipulative child who whines that he is unhappy because Mommy didn't fix his favorite meal, or Dad didn't play with him right when he wanted. Or a friendly neighbor suggests that you give in to a teen's demand for "no curfew" because to do otherwise is to incur your child's wrath. Or a college son complains that he is the only guy in his apartment that does not have a car, and he is very unhappy. The message is that if you are a "good parent," you will keep your child happy.

Being happy is a great blessing in life. But sometimes we confuse momentary "happiness" (having what we want when we want it to its fullest extent) with long-term peace, satisfaction, and joy.

Is happiness the ultimate goal in life? Is doing what will make our children happy always the right course of action? Is trying always to

---

Our job as parents is not to make our children happy. Naturally, we want happiness for our children, but this cannot be our primary goal, because the result will be an unhappy self-centered person.

---

insulate our children from sadness, disappointment, or loneliness the wisest thing? Loneliness might be the result of having made a courageous choice not to follow the crowd. Disappointment may be an important factor in learning patience. Failure in some area may be God's way of directing us to another area in life in which we will find deep fulfillment and satisfaction. The things that your child may feel he or she needs "to be happy" are sometimes the very opposite of what he or she needs in order to mature and learn compassion or integrity or selflessness. Difficulty hardly ever produces happiness in the short run, but difficult experiences often are vitally important in shaping character.

A parent never wants to cause a child to be unhappy. But a wise parent will remember that he is building for the future. Just "being happy" is too shortsighted, too immature a goal.

A second inadequate goal which we often strive toward is success.

Success means very different things to different people. Some see success as having the independent means to do whatever you want in life. Some see it in terms of career accomplishments.

How do you define *success?* When or how will you know that you have become a success? Consider this: When you have died and your family and friends are together attending your funeral, what things about you do you want your loved ones to remember? What heritage do you want to pass on to them? Do you want to be remembered for your achievements? For your influence? For the organization you started or the long hours you worked?

One man who came to me for marriage counseling said, when asked what were his goals in life, "I want to be the best stockbroker in the city and the best tennis player in the state." That was his idea of what it means to be a success. Have you really considered carefully what success means for you?

Sometimes we are so fully occupied with all the challenges of work, family, church, and community life that we lose track of how the culture in which we are living is changing. One area in which westerners have undergone a subtle shifting in outlook is in the area of how we view success.

During the first one hundred fifty years or so of our nation's history, Americans thought of success in terms of character. Hundreds of books, articles, and essays were published; one of the most famous is Ben Franklin's autobiography. The chief emphasis was the necessity of becoming people of character. Basic to the way of thinking was the conviction that both happiness and success in life are directly related to becoming a person who is honest and kind, industrious and good. Fairness, moderation, and courage were stressed repeatedly as essential in life.[1]

But since World War II, we have observed a rather drastic change of thought in the area of what it means to be successful. A predominant theme in much literature implies that success is having your own way. To achieve what you want in life is, for many, the object of life. Along with this is an emphasis on personality instead of character. We learn how to influence people through our personality, through communication techniques, and through psychological insights. Body language and facial expression are crucially important. While many of these insights have been helpful, the underlying idea of manipulation in order to attain one's desired goals is alarming. The "photo opportunity" has become almost more important than the hard work needed to effectively grapple with this or that problem. We fear that our leaders are more concerned with appearance than substance.

Is this success? Saying the right thing, looking, on the surface, like a caring human being while in reality being self-focused and chiefly concerned to reach your personal goals? No, this is superficiality. My wife and I recognize it in others and want to avoid it in ourselves and our children.

Wealth, power, position—these are goals which, even when achieved, are awfully difficult to keep. This sort of success is fleeting at best. And now we are beginning to pay the price of an unhealthy focus upon materialism in our society. The get-rich-quick philosophy has backfired. We are becoming in the words of T. S. Eliot, "hollow men."

Finally, our Western culture realizes that a life devoted chiefly to obtaining position and power over others, to gathering up material things and making money, a life solely devoted to the pursuit of one's career development can lead to emotional, moral, and spiritual poverty, to empty self-indulgence, and to depression. Our nation has perhaps reached the pinnacle or the limits of the sort of success which materialism provides only to discover how shallow it all is. This is the dark side of success.

A person bent on satisfying his own selfish desires becomes empty at the core. A life all wrapped up in oneself makes a very small package.

The pursuit of material success has brought us to a point of ethical disarray as a people. The latter twentieth-century American has witnessed unethical excesses in government and business that were undreamed of earlier in this century. We have attacked these illegalities with presidential commissions, congressional inquiries, and expensive armies of lawyers, as well as with our own public indignation. But we are confused in our morality. Our most prestigious universities flounder in discomfort when asked to develop courses to steer our future leaders through the difficult moral issues before them. Ethics professors cannot agree as to whose ethics to embrace, so we drift morally. This is not meant to be a book on ethics, but it is a book about character and is based upon the premise that the best foundation for character is the biblical teaching of the Judeo-Christian tradition. The moral example of character most worthy of emulation is Jesus Himself.

Since happiness and success in themselves are not adequate, we look beyond them and see a more substantial goal as individuals and as parents.

Our goal is to become confident people with deeply-rooted, Christ-centered values that equip us for living a life of integrity before God and in service to our fellowman. It follows that our responsibility as parents is to equip our children with the character necessary to live a life pleasing to God.

My wife and I are parents writing primarily to other parents who know that their own character will do much to shape that of their children. We write for parents who have accepted that there is a culture around us that we must counter on behalf of our children in order to help them learn to make the wisest and best decisions. At times it seems the culture, with its vast array of options, will overwhelm us. We do not want to become negative people, contrary head-shaking parents always wearing a face that says no around our children. Yet, we realize there is a constant need to guard ourselves and our loved ones against a culture that says yes to almost everything except to saying no. We want to be wise, loving, and positive parents, and we believe that we can be but know we need some encouragement and advice from time to time. It seems like an uphill battle at times, however, because many are confused by what the word *character* means. What is *character?* How can we see our own character and that of our children molded into maturity?

SHAPING CHARACTER

Although there are several factors that shape the development of a person's character, it is generally agreed that parents are the fundamental key to the development of their children's character. We have the responsibility and the privilege to help our children learn to be outstanding men and women. We teach them in the ordinary activities of the day-to-day life we share. Other caring adults can play important roles in the shaping of our children, but the influence of family on character cannot be overemphasized.

A well-known example is that of two New England families, the Jukes and the Edwards. Max Jukes and Jonathan Edwards both lived in the state of New York over two hundred years ago. Jonathan Edwards was a pastor and is known to have at least nine hundred twenty-nine descendants. Of these, four hundred thirty were ministers, eighty-six became university professors, thirteen became university presidents, seventy-five wrote good books, five were elected to the United States Congress and two to the Senate. One was vice president of the United States. As far as we know, the descendants of this family did not cost the state of New York one cent but contributed immeasurably to the life and strength of not only New York but also of our nation.

Max Jukes was a contemporary of Jonathan Edwards who spent a good deal of his life in the prisons of New York. He was not known to be a Christian and did not expose his children to church, even when they asked to go. He is known to have had at least one thousand twenty-six descendants. Three hundred were sent to prison for an average of thirteen years, one hundred ninety were public prostitutes, six hundred eighty were admitted alcoholics. His family has cost the state of New York hundreds of thousands of dollars and does not appear to have made much contribution to society.[2]

This radical example of family dysfunction gone rampant down through the generations is a gross statement of the impact of parents and family members upon present and future generations. In our day, people are crying out for help, for healing from the hurts and habits of the home like never before.

In the home, in the family, and in the daily humdrum of ordinary life, our moral character is shaped. We become the sort of persons our friends will remember, not necessarily on the mountain top but down on the monotonous plains.

What is character?

Character, in its most basic sense, is simply the essential quality of something, the essence of what something or someone is made. But we are using the word in this book to describe the moral constitution of someone—the inner quality of an individual which issues in behavior, or what determines whether a person will behave in an honorable way or a dishonorable way. It is what we are really like when all the veneers are stripped away, what we are like when no one is around and no one is looking and no one will find out.

When we get down to our character, the question we must ask is: Is there true virtue there? Is there goodness and moral excellence? Or is there moral weakness and internal corruption?

As we reflect on this subject of character we realize that there are different character types that might be summarized as expedient, malleable, legalistic, and principled.

The Expedient Character

Expediency means doing what works best to get what one wants instead of doing what is right. This person almost always behaves in a self-centered way, doing exactly what he or she wants in the pursuit of self-gratification. Adherence to a moral code is clearly a secondary concern and is important only in order to keep oneself out of trouble with the authorities. A young child generally behaves this way until family guidance and example begins to take effect.

The Malleable Character

This person has no firmly set character but is molded by those around him. He or she is the type who often wants to please other people. Acceptance and approval determine moral behavior more than any deep-seated internal sense of right and wrong. A young child will begin to tell the truth and exhibit the sort of behavior his or her parents desire, at first, in order to please them and avoid a spanking rather than because the child has matured.

The Legalistic Character

This is the person who carefully lives his or her life according to an external set of rules or laws. Doing the right thing is a matter of obedience to the laws which have been established. The *why* of a certain form of behavior may not have been grasped, but the outward habits have certainly been established. A child may adhere precisely to his parents' guidelines without really grasping the underlying principles.

The Principled Character

This person, whose character is the most maturely developed, has come to the place where he or she lives a life in keeping with the moral values that have been presented to the child over and over again. But she lives a good life not just because this is what she has been taught, or because this is what the law requires, but rather because deep inside she has learned the sound reasons which underlie the life-style her parents taught her. She understands the concept of truth and believes in it; therefore, she seeks to tell the truth. She understands the value of the person and therefore exhibits courtesy and compassion. Behavior is not based simply on outward conformity with the law or with the family's own teachings of what is considered right behavior. Decisions are made, actions taken, and lines drawn because they grow out of a deep sense of integrity, fairness, commitment to others, commitment to God, and out of a deep inner respect for principles that are worth upholding and maintaining no matter what. The person who lives this way has a mature, thoughtful character.[3]

Clearly it is an oversimplification to generalize with these four character types, but they are good examples of different types of people. As we analyze different varieties of character, we find ourselves wondering just where does a person's character come from? How is the principled

---

Strong, true moral character is not simply a matter of environment, family background, parental and peer influence, and hard work. Character is of utmost concern to our Creator as well.

---

person produced? How can we ourselves become more truly principled people, and how can we help our children and our neighbors' children become men and women of character?

THE CREATOR'S CONCERN FOR CHARACTER

One final point: Strong, true moral character is not simply a matter of environment, family background, parental and peer influence, and hard work. Character is of utmost concern to our Creator as well. The God who gave us life is both the definition and the ultimate source of genuine goodness. Anyone, whatever his or her background, can develop character. Any child, however wayward, can grow into a fine person. Jesus always viewed people from the perspective not just of what they were but of what *they could become.* He believed in the new birth, beginning again, forgiveness, and regeneration.

When a person opens his life up to the reality of God and embraces the principles and promises of Jesus, giving himself as wholly as he is capable to the God who made him, this opens the way for the Spirit of

God to set about shaping his interior life, the divine process the church calls *sanctification* and which we describe here as *character development*.

God Himself becomes our partner in the whole process, and as we learn to depend upon Him, trust Him, and obey Him, He shapes our souls. We don't do it all alone. He enables us and our children to grow and to become so much better than we are.

All of us are people in process, and none of us has attained full moral character, maturity, and consistency. Hardly a day goes by that we do not realize, if we are ruthlessly honest with ourselves, how easily we ourselves succumb to excuse-making, expediency, selfishness, and trickery. But however inconsistent we may be, it is not too late to begin to grow again.

Many of us have been adversely affected as a result of growing up in dysfunctional family systems. The outpouring of literature over the last several years dealing with the overcoming of dysfunction has been helpful to many.

This book is offered for the person who has begun to make some progress toward recovering wholeness and will encourage the person who has concluded that he will do his best not to repeat the mistakes of the past generation, but will instead embark on establishing new and healthy patterns for himself and his family. This is a book to help you take your family in a healthy, new direction, to begin to write a new script, and to establish new, wise, and good patterns of family life.

If you were fortunate enough to grow up in a healthy home, this book will reinforce principles learned in your youth and provide fresh applications to the challenges of today.

In the following chapters we explore eight traits which are essential to becoming families of character: integrity, a teachable spirit, self-discipline, compassion, a servant's heart, courage, faith, and joy.

You will benefit most if you read this book one chapter at a time, allowing time to reflect on the material, study the questions, and determine what actions you want to take in your own family. The book is also designed to be used by couples or in small groups, and a leader's guide is available in Appendix 3.

My wife and I invite you to come with us as we pursue the meaning and the making of these qualities of character in our own lives and in the lives of our children.

FOCUS QUESTIONS

Meditate on Hebrews 11:23–28

1. How do you see genuine character manifested in the life of the parents as well as in the man Moses?

2. Take a few minutes to consider your parents or other family members who have had a deep impact on the shaping of your character. What qualities in their lives have you most clearly accepted as being quite important to your value system?

3. The prophet Micah wrote, "He has told you, O man, what is good; And what does the LORD require of you but to do justice, to love kindness, and to walk humbly with your God?" (Micah 6:8).

   • If you were going to describe in a similar manner the three qualities you think are most important to God, what would they be?

   • If you could be remembered for three particular qualities by others after your death, what would they be? What qualities do you most want to help your children cultivate?

Meditate on Psalm 139:23–24. As you begin to study this book make this your own prayer, writing it out in your own words.

*Moreover, I will give you a new heart
and put a new spirit within you; and I will
remove the heart of stone from your flesh and give you
a heart of flesh. And I will put My Spirit within you and
cause you to walk in My statutes, and you will be
careful to observe my ordinances.
(Ezekiel 36:26–27)*

INTEGRITY
(Susan)

TWO

*I hope I shall possess firmness and virtue enough
to maintain what I consider the most enviable of all titles,
the character of an honest man.*

GEORGE WASHINGTON

*P*iercing screams of anger brought an abrupt end to our pleasant conversation.

"Oh no," groaned my friend Sarah. "They're at it again."

As if on cue, a red-faced, teary-eyed four-year-old ran into the room with his seven-year-old sister at his heels.

"He kicked me!" blurted out Annie, anxious to get in the first word. Little Joe's sobs only intensified as he looked up at his mother.

"Son, did you kick your sister?" asked Sarah wearily.

"Y-y-yes," wailed the distressed child, "but she bit me first."

"No, I didn't," challenged Annie, in her know-it-all big sister manner.

"Yes, you *did*," sobbed Joe.

"Annie," Sarah commanded firmly, "look at me. Now. Did you bite your brother?"

Unable to avoid her mother's knowing eyes, Annie stammered indignantly,

"Well *maybe* my teeth *might* have *accidentally* bumped into his arm, but I don't know. I can't help it if that was an accident. And how am I supposed to keep track of what my teeth are doing anyway?"

This particular incident made me dissolve in laughter at little Annie's creative rationalization. Flashbacks of my own children in similar situations came quickly to mind. In Annie I also saw myself and my instinctive desire for self-preservation—at any cost.

Each of us can identify with Annie. It is so much easier to lie or at least to make excuses for our behavior by blaming someone or something else. After all, we don't want to face punishment, and *this small act is not that big a deal anyway.*

We most often shade the truth in the little things. "Surely it won't make that much difference," we reason. "After all, this is only a little thing." Yet, it is in the small areas of life that the big lessons are learned, and the principle of integrity provides us with the clearest example of this.

BUILDING INTEGRITY

Integrity means more than just honesty; it is a larger word with a broader meaning. Integrity involves trustworthiness, objectivity, fairmindedness, sincerity, scrupulousness, thoroughness. It means soundness all the way through. A person of integrity is genuine—what you see is what you get, no pretense, no sham.

To live with integrity is to live by the highest standard—a standard that calls for complete honesty, an honesty that encourages a consistency of values. Personal perfection is impossible, but it is possible to aim for genuineness, honesty, consistency and moral purity, and to frankly acknowledge it when we fail. A person of integrity doesn't seek to cover up or make excuses when he fails.

Integrity doesn't necessarily mean good or bad, right or wrong. Rather, it implies a sense of purity. Gold that is considered pure has no other substances. Glass that is clear has no distortions. There is a sense of complete consistency in something that is pure.

Years ago the cover of the *New York Herald Tribune* Sunday magazine showed a photo of the Statue of Liberty taken from above, presumably from a helicopter. The amazing thing about the top of the Lady of Liberty's head was that every inch of the hair and crown was worked out in perfect detail. When the sculptor did this incredible work in the 1800s, airplanes had not yet been invented. Thus, the artist thought that only he and perhaps sea gulls would ever view this portion of the monument. Yet he spent as much time on this "hidden" part of the work as he did on the face or the feet or the folds of the dress. That's consistency. That's integrity.

Our goal for ourselves and for our children is for integrity to become an instinct. It is not so much determining "to do" something else

---

Personal perfection is impossible, but it is possible to aim for genuineness, honesty, consistency and moral purity, and to frankly acknowledge it when we fail. A person of integrity doesn't seek to cover up or make excuses when he fails.

---

in our lives or in the lives of our kids as it is to choose "to be" something different. I want to be a person of integrity, and that means that I will seek to be honest and consistent in all of my attitudes and actions.

But won't that lead to hypocrisy? What happens when we fail? How can my husband and I expect our children to live up to a standard that we fail in ourselves?

Hypocrisy is not caused by high standards, but by parents who wink at the standards for themselves while insisting on adherence by their children. Genuine integrity, on the other hand, maintains a high standard while acknowledging failure and seeking to grow.

Integrity produces freedom rather than bondage. There is no need to pretend to be someone or something that I am not. Instead, I have confidence in who I am. I know the standard that I have set, and I realize that growing in integrity is a lifelong process marked by failures and victories.

We have a little farm nestled in the hills at the edge of the Blue Ridge Mountains of Virginia. On hot summer days, one of our favorite activities is to go for a swim in the cool, fresh water of our pond. Were you to drive up the dusty, old country road by our place you would hear squeals of delight coming from the direction of the water. Great splashes would catch your attention, and you might see two children desperately trying to balance on a large truck inner tube in the middle of the water.

Before we had the farm, I never imagined that maintaining a pond took work. Now I know differently. Each spring, when swimming time is fast approaching, several of us climb into the canoe and paddle around the pond to collect algae that has spread out of control. We also have to clean out areas where the neighborhood beaver has built his house. Recently we discovered that we have a large snapping turtle that is eating our fish. Now the challenge is to catch that irritating turtle. We have to get rid of him because we need the fish. And it is intimidating to swim with a snapping turtle. There are always things we have to get out of the pond.

Not only do we need to get things out of the pond, there are some things that my husband and I must put into it in order to maintain it. Carp fish, for example, are necessary because they eat the algae. Fresh water pouring down the mountain into the mouth of the pond is necessary to keep the water flowing clean. John had to put in a drainpipe to prevent flooding and control water flow. *Cleaning out* and *putting in* are both necessary for a healthy pond.

In a similar way, there are several ingredients that need to be "put in" and several that need to be "taken out" in order to help develop the quality of integrity.

Four ingredients necessary to "build into" a person of integrity are: humility, consistency, trustworthiness, and honesty.

Humility

A humble person is first of all a person without pretense—someone who seems comfortable with himself. A humble person doesn't have to pretend to "be something" to impress someone. Rarely would he have to be the center of attention at a party. Instead, there is a genuineness about the person.

Our home should be the first place where we live without pretense, where we are able to be natural with one another. Ask yourself, *Is our home a place where we are real or where we pretend?* As parents we set the tone of naturalness or pretense in our home. When we create an environment of honest openness that encourages approachability and loving acceptance, we discourage pretense and encourage humility.

Several weeks ago, our family was on vacation at my brother-in-law's home. My brother-in-law, Tucker, had been having a tough time in his business. One evening when my husband and I talked with Tucker and his wife Ginny, he began to share openly the painful struggles he was having in the business. He wondered if he had made some bad judgments. And he shared honestly the pain of a difficult personnel problem. During the conversation, his twenty-year-old son pulled up a chair and quietly began to listen to our conversation. Tucker's openness continued as he wondered aloud what mistakes he had made and shared how he longed for God to change his attitudes. As our conversation drew to a close, we prayed for God to touch Tucker and to bring him through this difficult time. Tucker's openness before his son was completely natural. It was true humility, and his example will give his son the freedom to be open in return.

A person of humility will have the deep conviction that his attitudes and his actions are determined by God's standards rather than by the world's standards. God's standards for me spring out of His great love for me. He totally accepts me as His child. This does not mean that He approves of everything that I do, but it does mean that the standards He sets are motivated by love and are for my own good. He knows that I will fail, and He stands waiting to open His arms in forgiveness. Psalm 103:14 says that He knows that we are but dust. There is something very comforting in knowing that God realizes that I am but dust. He knows my frailty, and He understands. I don't have to pretend to be strong or to be right before God. He wants me to be humble.

As a child I remember my own dad saying to me, "Susan, I love you so much."

"Why?" I responded.

"Just because you are mine," he replied.

On another occasion he said to me, "No matter where you go in life or what you do, I will always be here for you or come to you wherever you are."

His love for me gave me a sense of belonging and security. His standards were high, and he was a firm disciplinarian. I was punished when I disobeyed, yet never did I fear rejection from him. His love communicated acceptance which encouraged humility.

A sense of humility will allow us to be open about our strengths and our weaknesses in two ways. First, humility enables us to be honest about the things we are good at as well as those areas in which we are not so good. Second, humility makes it easier for us to acknowledge the areas in which we are tempted as well as those where it is easier to stand strong. These will be different for each person.

I love good music, but I cannot carry a tune. My children are constantly embarrassed when I try to sing. I am the one family member who would never be asked to join a choir! I do, however, have good organizational skills and am able to use these abilities in the family as well as in the church.

John isn't very good with figures. Getting the checkbook to balance is a great burden for him. I'm not much better, but it relieves him if I do it. He's got a great sense of humor about his inability to balance things, and the children laugh with him.

As parents it is important for us to communicate to our children that they do not have to be the best at everything. They, too, will be good at some things and lousy at others. When we are honest about ourselves, we create an atmosphere in which our children can be objective, too.

You may be tempted by beautiful things and struggle with materialism. This is not a particular area in which I am tempted. Instead, I struggle with the temptation to worry rather than to trust. If one of my teens is late, I'm sure he's been in an accident. My fertile imagination can create the most ghastly traffic accident. Frequently I have to go to God, confessing my worrying heart and asking Him to help me grow in trusting Him more. My children know this weakness of mine and help me by calling if they are going to be late.

A close friend of mine has struggled for many years with a weight problem. In particular, it is very hard for her to resist the temptation of chips and breads. Sometime ago she shared her discouragement with her family. They decided that to help her they would no longer keep chips or breads in the house. My friend's honesty with her family caused them to make a small sacrifice in order to help her with her temptations.

A home where family members are open about their strengths, weaknesses, and temptations will be a home that is cultivating a spirit of humility. And integrity will blossom in the home where failure is permitted but encouragement is generously given.

Consistency

A person growing in integrity will be a person who strives for consistency in his life. My standards of behavior should be the same no matter what I do.

As a minister's wife, I am often asked, "Isn't it hard being the wife of a minister? You have to be good all the time, and your children's behavior must be exemplary."

Actually, my life-style has nothing to do with my husband's profession. I live the way I do, not because of my husband's job, but because of my faith in Christ. The world may have different standards for those

---

A home where family members are open about their strengths, weaknesses, and temptations will be a home that is cultivating a spirit of humility. And integrity will blossom in the home where failure is permitted but encouragement is generously given.

---

in "full-time ministry," yet God's expectations dictate how we live. I would not change my standards or raise my children any differently if my husband were a lawyer or a grocer. Living under God's standards encourages a spirit of consistency because we are responding to a loving heavenly Father rather than to a fickle world.

Consistency will be illustrated in the way in which we live and in the way in which we treat others.

We should not have one personality on Sundays and another on Mondays, one personality with Christian friends and another with the folks at the office. Our behavior toward those socially or professionally, our peers and our behavior toward those who work for us, should be the same. We should treat our children with the same attitude of respect and thoughtfulness that we would our best friend.

A friend of mine once worked for an executive of what she described as a Christian company. Her boss was well-respected in the community and had a wonderful ministry of caring for others. However, in the office her behavior toward my friend was intimidating, unkind, and rude. The young girl was treated with such disdain that she finally quit her job. Her boss's inconsistency demonstrated a lack of integrity.

Our five children were born in a span of seven years. When they were all small, I functioned in a state of constant fatigue. I remember one day driving in the car—with all the children—and being a totally grouchy mom. I warned my children that I was grouchy because I was tired. As we pulled into the gas station and I spoke to the attendant in a pleasant voice, one of my children turned to me and said, "Mommy, you weren't tired at him!" My inconsistency was showing, even to my tiny child!

Our children will learn consistency as they watch us relate to those around us. They know we are not perfect, and we know it, too. They don't need perfect parents but honest ones who are desiring to become consistent people. As we seek to grow in consistency it is helpful to ask several questions:

- Do I watch my language when I am at church or Bible study and then let loose at home?
- Do I treat the woman who cleans my office in the same manner that I treat my business partner? Do I genuinely care for her?
- Do I speak to my mate or my child in the same manner that I would my friend?

A family that is growing in consistency will be a family that is growing in integrity.

Trustworthiness

Recently I had a problem and I needed a friend to talk to. So I picked up the phone and called Ann, a person with whom I can speak freely. She is wise and often gives me sound advice. I know that when I share with her, she will keep my confidences. She is trustworthy and would never be called a gossip. I have never heard her talk about anyone else.

Keeping confidences is an important ingredient in becoming a trustworthy person.

If we want our children to learn to keep confidences, we must take care not to become people who gossip. If we want them to share freely with us, they must have the confidence that they will not hear their problem repeated by their best friend's mother.

But what do we do about small children and secrets? We want our children to learn to keep confidences, but sometimes they may try to keep a secret which really needs to be told. Perhaps your young child saw her older brother smoking marijuana, and she was warned not to tell. Obviously, the parents need to know this "secret" about their son's problem in order to obtain help before his problems get worse.

A good rule of thumb to share with children is, "Keep a secret unless it can be harmful to the person or to someone else. Then you must tell an adult. Even if you know the person will get angry, it is better to tell."

Sometimes secrets can be used to promote cliques. Eight-year-old girls can be brutal in telling secrets which leave other children out. "Sarah and I have secret code words, and we're not telling Beth. Then she won't play with us." Or they may even say, "Beth, we have a secret, and we aren't telling you!"

These types of secrets simply promote unkindness. We must help our children recognize the difference between good secrets and bad secrets.

Another aspect of becoming trustworthy is *growing in reliability*. Recently my son Chris asked me to hem a pair of his pants. I said I would do it. Even though I said each day that I would fix them, the pants sat on my "to do pile" for several days. Finally, in exasperation my son said, "Aw, Mom, I know you won't do them today."

It seemed to be such a small thing, but suddenly I realized that I was actually teaching my son that I was not trustworthy. If I had said, "Son, I can't do them today, but I will have them done by this weekend," that would have been different. Instead, each day I said that I would fix them, and I did not come through. My procrastination gave my son the impression that I was unreliable.

We never intend to teach our children that we are unreliable, but sadly this can be the underlying message we communicate by our behavior or lack of it. When our children feel they can't count on us, they become frustrated.

The small, everyday issues of life teach the lessons of integrity. In the small issues, our children pick up our values that will influence how they deal with the big issues in life.

Honesty

Not long ago, *Time* magazine asked on its cover, "Are we becoming a nation of liars?"

The implied answer was yes. People are thinking and writing about these matters in our country, but the thinking is more analytical than prescriptive. We frankly seem rather confused about truth telling.

Mary Ann Mason Ekman, in her book, *Why Kids Lie*, tells of analyzing her own conduct for a week after becoming upset with her teenage son who had lied about a party. She found that she wasn't above reproach either, catching herself in no less than eight lies, two of them to her children. About this, she later said, "These were all lies of convenience, lies I didn't need to tell."[1]

Implicit in this statement seems to be the idea that some lies are necessary. And yet this is one quality about which the Bible is quite clear. Jesus felt so strongly about our words that He even condemned the taking of oaths or swearing to tell the truth on the simple basis that our word should be enough to always be trusted. "Do not swear at all . . . simply let your 'Yes' be 'Yes' and your 'No,' 'No'" (Matthew 5:34a, 37, NIV).

In a world of half truths, we face the lifelong challenge of telling the whole truth even when it's inconvenient. Our desire to be good parents should cause us to want to be truthful. After all, I must strive to be honest if I want my children to be honest.

In my own life, I have been challenged by the temptation to exaggerate. But in striving to raise honest kids, I have had to face my own weaknesses and be more careful to be accurate in my speech rather than to stretch the truth. I'm still working on it.

In our family, lying has always resulted in a strong punishment. The children know that it is far better to confess to a wrongdoing and be disciplined than to lie about it.

A roomful of four-year-olds would most likely tell you that being honest means don't lie. They may also add, don't steal and don't cheat.

When our daughter Libby was three, she took some candy from the grocery store. This provided a natural opportunity to explain to her how wrong it was to steal. Part of the lesson involved returning the candy to the store and apologizing.

Our children are surrounded by opportunities to cheat. From the family board games to the history quiz at school, there are plenty of chances. Notice your children at play. Correct attempts to cheat. Tell them how important it is to be honest. Assure them that you'd rather they do poorly on a quiz than copy someone else's work.

Our boys are currently playing on the varsity tennis team at school. One of the things I appreciate about their coach is that he demands that they make honest line calls. I would much rather they lose a point than be dishonest in a call. Our long-range goal is to build character. Tough calls in tennis are tools to build boys of integrity.

In addition to the more obvious, "Don't lie, steal, or cheat," which we use to define honesty, there is a more subtle aspect. That is *doing the*

In a world of half truths, we face the lifelong challenge of telling the whole truth even when it's inconvenient. Our desire to be good parents should cause us to want to be truthful. After all, I must strive to be honest if I want my children to be honest.

---

best I can in any particular job. My best may not be nearly as good as your best on a particular project, but my sense of personal integrity is well served when I do the best that I can.

The most obvious way we train our children is to help them learn to do the best they can on their homework. The best for one child might be a C, while for another it would be an A. As a child learns to take pride in a job well done he is growing in personal integrity.

Doing what is right is another aspect of honesty. Several years ago, we were in England with our children. Walking down the street from Piccadilly Circus, our son Chris noticed a bundle of money on the pavement. Reaching down, he picked up a rather large amount of foreign currency. *What wonderful luck*, we thought. But then we wondered about the person who dropped the money. We decided the right thing to do was to go to the nearest police station and turn it in—a tough choice for our eleven-year-old son. The police took his name and promised that if no one claimed the money within a month, they would mail it to him. He never got the money. A greater lesson was learned though. Chris had a sense that he had done what *he knew was right.*

Humility, consistency, trustworthiness, and honesty are each aspects that we need to build into our lives and the lives of our children if we want to be growing in integrity.

CLEANING OUT

Just as there were things to weed out of the pond, there are two things we need to clean out of our lives as we grow in integrity: *rationalization* and *misplaced blame.*

Rationalization

Perhaps the most dangerous force working against us as we desire to be people of integrity is rationalization. Today's litmus test for honesty seems to have become, "It's okay to do what you want to do so long as no one gets hurt or you don't get caught. Or if you get caught, it must be legally done or it doesn't count."

God's standard is that you do what's right when no one is looking and no one will find out.

As parents we are quick to discipline the child that tells a blatant lie. But how easy it is to slip into deception in our homes without even realizing it.

The phone rings, and our spouse doesn't want to talk to the person on the other end. It is so convenient simply to say that he's not in. Our child hasn't finished a paper and stays up late, oversleeping the next day. It is too embarrassing to tell the truth, so we simply call the school to say that our child isn't feeling well and will be late or absent. The cashier at the fast-food restaurant gives us too much change. We don't realize it until we are in the car. It's too much trouble to go back, so we pocket the money.

Each of these examples seems so petty, yet in the small everyday issues of life we have the greatest opportunity to grow in integrity ourselves and to show our children what honesty really means. Telling the unwelcome caller or the school the truth and returning the extra change will have a far greater impact on teaching our children integrity than any speech we give them. We must take care to guard against rationalization that whispers, "Everyone is doing it. It won't hurt anyone, and no one will find out."

For several years I have met weekly with a group of women to pray for our schools. We pray for our teachers, staff, and students. We pray for our children to be honest, and often we pray that if they are doing anything wrong they will get caught. Once, one of the children was caught giving answers to another child on a test. Her wise parents used this opportunity to emphasize their love for her and their commitment to raise her to be totally honest. For this child, getting caught became a positive learning experience in the importance of honesty.

On another occasion one of our sons and a buddy were throwing "dirt clods" at passing cars. They didn't "think" their antics would hurt anyone. After all, they rationalized, it was just harmless fun. But the first car they hit happened to be a police car. Quickly, the officer jumped out of his car and gave two thoroughly frightened young boys a firm scolding. Then he brought them home. The boys soon realized how lucky they were to have been caught before they caused an automobile accident. We had our son write a letter to the police officer to apologize and to thank him for catching them!

Being caught can become a great opportunity for growth. It will not be pleasant, yet it is a blessing in disguise. We will see how our ability to rationalize can lead us into trouble, and we will learn that being caught provides an opportunity to confess. Finally, we will be reminded that improper behavior has negative consequences.

Misplaced Blame

One day when I was potty-training the twins, I noticed that Libby had a strange look on her face and was walking in an awkward manner.

"Libby," I asked, "did you wet your pants?"

"No, Mommy," she replied. "Susy did it!"

At this particular moment I burst out laughing, but her response was so typical of each of us. Most children will attempt to blame others.

"She made me do it," will be heard frequently in a household of young children. My sister Fran has found it helpful to ask her children the question, "Who are *you* responsible for?" This question serves as a reminder that we are responsible for our own behavior.

Our natural instincts will often be to blame others—our parents, our boss, our circumstances.

I've noticed that misplaced blame sometimes comes disguised as the "If Onlys"—if only my parents had had a good marriage, if only my husband were more affectionate or didn't work such long hours, if only we had more money. The list is endless. Indulging ourselves in a case of the "If Onlys" is very easy.

Blaming others will only prevent us from growing in integrity. We must guard against this in our lives, for our children will quickly learn how to blame others if they sit at the dinner table and hear Mom or Dad blaming someone else.

Instead, we must accept responsibility and move on. Even if we have been unjustly treated, we should ask the question, "What would God teach me in this difficult situation that will help me grow closer to Him and produce within me a greater depth of integrity?"

HUNGER TO GROW

This spring our pond seems to need more work than ever. Slowly, a mass of gooey green algae has spread out into the center of the water, and the kids are getting tangled in it when they dive off the pier. In order to clean it out, we've been taking turns loading the old canoe with the slimy stuff and dumping it on the banks. More fish are needed to eat these annoying plants. And we've heard that if we put in a special ingredient called blue stone, the algae's growth will be retarded. Alas, there is constant work in maintaining a healthy pond.

Becoming people of integrity is a constant process that is never completed, involving "building in" good qualities and "weeding out" bad ones. To do this, we simply need a genuine desire. As parents, we must have a deep hunger within ourselves to grow in this area. Our children will always pick up on this hunger. As we desire to grow in integrity we might keep these four final thoughts in mind:

Hunger for righteousness. If we don't have a hunger, we can simply ask God to begin to give us one. Spending time in the Psalms and Proverbs each day will instill in us a hunger for righteousness. A friend of mine reads one psalm and one proverb every day, which has given her a hunger for righteousness.

Spend time with others who hunger. If we spend most of our time with people of questionable integrity, our desire for integrity will wane. On the other hand, when I am with someone whose life is admirable, I am challenged. Having good role models come into our home to visit with parents and children is one way of encouraging a hunger for righteousness.

Seek to please God, not impress people. Asking tough questions about my own motives will help me determine whom I am trying to please. What is my motive? Am I trying to elevate myself? Is this what God would want? What would Jesus say if He were here right now? Sometimes we use our jobs or our children to elevate ourselves. As we strive to please God, our children will learn that pleasing Him is most important of all.

Acknowledge failure and receive forgiveness. We must not be afraid of failure, nor too proud to admit our shortcomings. No matter how hard we try, we will fail and so will our children. Instead, we should look failure in the face and acknowledge it, knowing that in failure, we can begin to grasp the incredible power of God's forgiveness. God understands our weakness, and He knows our sin. We have only to admit our sins and ask Him for His forgiveness. Not only will He forgive us, but He will also give us the power to begin afresh.

FOCUS QUESTIONS

Meditate on Colossians 3:1–17

1. Is there an area in your life in which the quality of integrity is fragile? What specific actions should you take this week to begin to rectify the situation?

2. Thinking about each of your children, how are they doing in the development of integrity? What can you as a parent do to encourage this trait in each child?

Meditate on Psalm 86:11–13. Make this a prayer for each family member.

And He has said to me, "My grace is sufficient for you, for power is perfected in weakness." Most gladly, therefore, I will rather boast about my weaknesses, that the power of Christ may dwell in me.
(2 Corinthians 12:9–10)

A TEACHABLE SPIRIT
(Susan)

THREE

And if on consideration, one can find no faults
on one's own side, then cry for mercy; for this must be
a most dangerous delusion.

C. S. LEWIS

I believe the first test of a truly great man is his humility.

JOHN RUSKIN

*A*n unusually cool, foggy August night shrouded the hillside beyond the old screened porch where my husband and I and two of our dearest pals were catching up on the summer's events in each other's lives. The warmth of the fellowship and the repeated laughter, not to mention the candles between us on the old wooden porch table, were more than enough to offset the chill of the night. John asked our friend how his mother was doing, or more precisely how was he doing with his mom. (It wasn't always an easy relationship.) He caught us off guard when he said, "Well, do you remember when I asked your mom for advice? She told me to stop trying to change my mother and just love and accept her the way she is. I told my wife the day after your mother gave us that advice that I thought she was dead wrong and crazy too, but as it has turned out, I was the one who was dead wrong."

You don't often hear a man like this admit that he's been wrong. Our love for him grew even a little bit stronger that night just for that reason—he didn't mind admitting that in his own normal, bullheaded way, he had been totally wrong. There's something powerfully important in this principle.

You might not have thought about it in exactly this way, but inherent in strong character is what we have learned to describe as a teachable spirit.

In contrast, consider another man. This man is known as a leader who has influenced others. He claims that he simply wants to use the many gifts and energies he has to do all that he can to help people come to faith and grow in the faith. He works hard and has many good insights as well as success in his work, but what has become so abundantly clear to me, and to some who have worked most closely with him, is that he does not show evidence of having a teachable spirit. He hasn't changed his mind about very much over the years. When he makes mistakes or fails to follow through on an obligation, I've noticed that, even though sometimes he will apologize, he then follows up with another comment that subtly shifts the blame to the shoulders of someone else. The man is not teachable, and that makes it difficult to work with or be friends with him. It is impossible for someone to grow if they are not aware that they need to grow and are not open to correction.

COMPONENTS OF A TEACHABLE SPIRIT

Have you ever noticed how hard it is for political leaders to admit they have been wrong? There seems to be a deep-seated mind-set that it is better to maintain one's original position and not budge even if it is more and more apparent that the stand is a wrong one. Sometimes the denial is very subtle. A simple statement, like "Poor judgment was used," instead of "*I* used poor judgment," is a subtle way of avoiding personal responsibility.

A teachable spirit begins with the realization that one is incomplete—intellectually, morally, and spiritually. None of us is all that we can be or need to be. The wise person wants to grow and is open to learn from anyone. Rather than seeking to justify his mistakes he wants to learn from them and therefore doesn't resent it when his errors or shortcomings are revealed.

The teachable person realizes that he or she is "in process" and has a long way to go, the very opposite of self-satisfaction.

Our information-based society hungers for more knowledge and information, but the person I'm describing hungers not so much for knowledge as for true wisdom. The teachable person is humble before God and deeply grateful for God's mercy upon his life. He realizes that he has done much in his life to incur God's anger, and instead of punishing him, God has blessed him beyond anything that he could ever

---

A teachable spirit begins with the realization that one is incomplete—intellectually, morally, and spiritually. None of us is all that we can be or need to be. The wise person wants to grow and is open to learn from anyone.

---

deserve. He goes through life with an underlying sense of thankfulness to God which enables God to develop in him the qualities of Christlikeness. The fruit of the Spirit—love, joy, peace, patience, kindness, goodness, gentleness, faithfulness, and self-control—can grow in the soil of a grateful heart but never in the soil of pride. A person with a heart filled with gratitude will be more likely to develop a teachable spirit.

Being teachable does not imply that one is a sniveling wimp just looking for somebody to straighten him out. Strength of personality and forceful opinions need not conflict with this quality. Some of the strongest people are also quite teachable because they know that as able as they may be, they still have much to learn.

We want to have a teachable spirit, and we want our kids to develop one. What components are there in a teachable spirit? How can we cultivate this spirit in our families?

Four components of a teachable spirit stand out:

- We value others
- We utilize discernment
- We appreciate perspective
- We hunger to grow

Value Others

"We reside in the most important city in the world." At least that is what the Riggs Bank commercial says. People living in the Washington, D.C., metropolitan area would most likely agree. Washington is the heartbeat of the nation. In its cramped conference rooms and expansive limousines, decisions are made daily that could impact the lives of every human. From the inner offices of the White House to a motel just outside the beltway, choices are being made which have tremendous ramifications. This is indeed a *power city.*

In this setting, you find a unique set of values. Your amount of influence over certain people determines your position, and tremendous importance is placed on position. There is a tendency to value those people who can help you move up the ladder, those who can introduce you to the right people, those who can sway opinion in your favor. Significance has become the basis of value. In essence, we come to value those who benefit us and we listen selectively to them.

How far this is from God's value system! To Him, each person is valuable, whether his office is in the west wing of the White House or the back room of the post office in Duffield Town, Virginia (population: fifty-four). Of course, we know this, and yet how easy it is to forget and to slip into the habit of placing a premium value on those who will benefit us.

If we want to cultivate a teachable spirit, we must recapture the sense that every person is valuable. When we live this way, we become open to learning from any person.

God may choose the most unlikely people to be His agents of training in our lives. Perhaps a young child will speak wisdom to an adult. Maybe a troublesome relative is to be God's tool in teaching us. His choice could be someone we wouldn't ordinarily notice.

A friend of ours, J. B., is a musician on the staff of a nearby church. He tells of being profoundly affected by the life of the church custodian, Virginia, a widow with no family. She lives in a rundown tenement house in a black neighborhood but works in a predominantly white, middle-class church.

Possessed with an unbridled devotion to the Lord and a passion for life, Virginia believes in doing everything right. Sloppiness is simply unacceptable to Virginia. Virginia's infectious enthusiasm has had a powerful impact on the entire membership of this church.

J. B. says that he has learned from watching and listening to Virginia that "no matter where you've been or who you are, there is some particular gift that God has given you." God has used this uneducated woman to bring perspective and hope to many people.

Accepting or Critical? When we value others, we choose to be open to whomever God puts in our lives. He may have something special that He wants to teach us through them. It is good to ask, "Am I open or closed to all those around me? Am I selective in those I value or am I open to God's choosing those through whom He would touch me?"

As we value others another question is pertinent: "Do I have an accepting or a critical spirit?"

John and I once knew a man who had a dynamic ministry. He was very effective in reaching many people for Christ. His own children loved the Lord, and through his life, much good was accomplished.

We enjoyed spending time with him, and yet I always felt a bit discouraged after being with him. He had a great sense of humor, but in nearly every conversation I noticed that he seemed to be critical of someone or some Christian organization. Subtly, he was always putting someone else down. Sometime later, we had the opportunity to spend time with his son. The son often appeared to be cynical and critical. He was not pleasant to be around, and he did not seem to have many close friends. His father would have been shocked to realize that he himself had a critical spirit. His motives were pure, and he truly loved the Lord, yet his subtle criticism had been picked up by his son, who had become a critical, negative person.

Observing this situation has caused me to check my own attitudes and speech. The family dinner table is a good place to do this. Reflecting on conversations around the meal, I occasionally ask myself, *Was I critical of anyone or any group? Did I put someone down in my conversation? Does my speech reflect that I am an accepting person or a person with a critical spirit?*

Of course, we must be people of discernment, yet there is a difference between evaluating and being critical. It is all too easy to unknowingly fall into the habit of criticizing. Our children will surely mimic this.

There are no perfect people and no perfect churches. Someone once said, "If you find a perfect church, don't join it. You'll ruin it."

Remembering that we don't have all the facts about a person's situation enables us to give them the benefit of doubt. We must determine to believe the best about others. When we as parents focus on people's gifts rather than exposing their faults, our children will be more likely to avoid the development of a critical spirit.

Two teenagers were overheard discussing another friend. "She's so unfriendly and cynical, no wonder people think she's a snob," remarked one of the girls.

"You're right," the second agreed. "But maybe she's really just shy, and it comes across as unfriendliness. Have you noticed how generous she is? I heard she gave some of her baby-sitting money to help a kid go to camp. And last week she gave Beth her own green sweater just because Beth had admired it for so long. She's really generous."

Learning to look for the good in someone and turning conversations in positive directions are good habits to cultivate. Our attitude should be that each person has a gift that we should learn from and encourage.

Talker or Listener? Another question to ask ourselves in considering how to value others is, *Am I a talker or a listener?*

My husband and I have two friends whom I'll call Jeff and Dave. Both are outgoing attractive men. Both have reached high positions in their professions, and both seek to follow Christ.

Jeff and Dave are good talkers and have interesting insights. Jeff, however, talks all the time and seems to need to be the focus of attention. He thrives on having peers laugh at his jokes and listen to his wisdom. Rarely does he ask anyone else's opinion or simply inquire how they are doing. Dave, on the other hand, makes it a point to ask personal questions. He wants to hear your opinions, and he is genuinely interested in you as a person. Guess who we'd rather spend an evening with! Dave, of course.

What makes Dave a good listener? He has developed sharp conversational skills. He asks good questions. Educator Chuck Miller suggests that when you can't think of anything to talk about, consider the topics of *schedules* and *relationships*.

Sitting next to someone you don't know at a dinner party can be an awkward situation. Embarrassing silence begins to stretch on and on. "What can I talk about?" Schedules and relationships. Every person, young and old, has a daily routine and specific people in his life.

"What is a typical day like for you at the office? What type of things have you been working on?" we might inquire of an adult.

A young person might be asked, "What subject do you like best in school? Whom do you enjoy spending time with?"

We've shared these two words, *schedules* and *relationships*, with our children and helped them think of sample conversation starters. They are encouraged to know that Mom and Dad sometimes feel awkward and that we have to work on our own communication skills.

"I would like your opinion" is another question that encourages listening skills, communicating to the person that we value what they think. Our self-confidence grows when we sense that other people value us.

Allison, our collegian, has a great eye for clothes. Instinctively she knows what looks good together and what does not. More and more I find that I need her opinion when I go shopping. I value her judgment, and she knows it.

We've noticed that John III (age sixteen) has a keen insight into people. After a meeting recently in our home, we asked John for his observations. With his shrewd insight, he noticed some things which neither of his parents did. Asking his opinion encourages the development of his insights.

When we desire to know our children's opinions about things, we communicate to them that we value them. Their self-worth grows when they know they are valued.

A person developing listening skills will also be one who says, "I'm wrong, you're right."

It's easy to say that and tack on a "but you" or "if you." This simply puts the blame on another's shoulders, and once again we avoid admitting that we were wrong.

When we truly value others, we recognize that we are often wrong in our own judgments. When was the last time you said to your wife, your coworker, or your child, "You are right; I am wrong"?

Pride prevents us from becoming good listeners. Choosing to value others enables us to be taught by them.

Utilize Discernment

Walk into your local bookstore and notice the abundance of "how to" books available to tell us how we should live. John and I once counted the billboards on a train trip between Washington and New York City and were amazed at the number of different products we *had* to have to live successfully or happily. In this era of media blitz, many different voices cry out to us telling us how to live. No wonder we are confused. How easy it becomes to give into the most persuasive voice.

Our problem is two-fold: *How do we choose between good and evil, and how do we make wise decisions with so many options?*

One would think that it would be easy to discern good from evil, but often the issue is not so clear. Good and evil are often camouflaged by the muddy waters of language.

What about making the right decision in the face of many alternatives? A friend of mine went through the exhausting trial of three moves in three years. She is a single parent and simply could not decide where she should locate after her divorce. There were many valid reasons for several different locations, and she couldn't decide what to do. Now, decision making is not her strong suit, but she did her best. She made an unwise decision, and the following year moved again. Many valuable lessons were learned in the process, but a filter through which to sift her alternatives would have saved her many headaches.

A coffee filter in my electric coffeemaker has an important job. After the hot water has flowed through the coffee, then it sifts away those unnecessary grounds and leaves a clear, delicious cup of black coffee. In a similar way, our families need a filter through which we can sift our thoughts in making decisions. God's Word and God's priorities are our filters in learning how to discern between good and evil and how to make wise decisions.

If we want to obey the Word of God, we must know what it says. There is no better way to know God's heart than to become intimately acquainted with His Word. Studying the Scriptures and applying them to our lives is the foundation to knowing what is good and what is evil. God never leads contrary to what He has already said in Scripture.

A man falls in love with a woman. He is a believer and knows that God's Word teaches that he should not have sex with her until they are married. But he loves her. How easy it is to persuade himself that God understands and doesn't want him to be miserable; therefore, God must be leading them to consummate the relationship *now*. That's not God leading. He has already spoken.

The foundation for knowing what is good and what is evil is found in the Scriptures. God's teaching always springs out of His great love for us—a love that wants the very best for us. So if we want to learn to

---

Making wise moral decisions is not always so simple as saying, "What does the Bible say about it?"... The process of discerning the best course of action often involves careful thought, discussion, prayer, Scripture, common sense, and the insights of wiser Christians of the past and present.

---

discern between good and evil, we must begin with the Word of God. When we uphold the Word as the authority in our life, our children will cultivate this same respect.

Making wise moral decisions is not always so simple as saying, "What does the Bible say about it?" Would that life were so easy! The process of discerning the best course of action often involves careful thought, discussion, prayer, Scripture, common sense, and the insights of wiser Christians of the past and present. Yet in the home, the study and discussion of the Scripture begins when our children are small and is a vital part of establishing the necessary foundation upon which decisions will be made the rest of their lives. There's no way to write apart from the foundation of the alphabet. In the same way, the Word of God is absolutely integral to discernment.

As we study Scripture, we have found that God seems to teach three priorities which are relevant for each of us.

- Our top priority is to love the Lord our God with all our heart, soul and mind. Thus, our first responsibility is to do all that we can to grow in our own relationship with Christ. This involves spending time in His Word, in prayer, and in fellowship with other believers.

- Our second priority is to love our neighbor. If we have a family they are our first "neighbors." Other neighbors would be close fellow believers.
- Our third priority is to be faithful in doing our best in the work that God has called us to do. No matter what our profession is, God has chosen us to be the salt of the earth and to help others come to know Him (Matthew 5:13-16).

When I have to distinguish between right and wrong, I look to God's Word. When I have to make a decision, I often think through how the decision will affect my priorities. Will this help me in my walk with Christ? Will this opportunity place my children in a situation where they can grow in their faith? Will I be better able to do Gods work in this new position?

Take advantage of the times you struggle with decisions. Share with a child the issues involved and the process you are going through to make a choice. Let him know that you look to God's Word for guidance; show him particular passages. Talk with your children of other things that you consider in decision making. John once drew up a list of "Ten Steps to Aid in Decision Making." You can find them in Appendix 2.

Talking about priorities with your children is a part of equipping them for decision making in their own lives. A good test is to ask your children what they think are your priorities. Young ones may not see clearly, but you'd be amazed at how close they come. Sometimes our lives have revealed that a wrong priority has entered in or that a priority has been lost. A good example is when our commitment to our professions replaces our commitment to our family. It is easy to spend more and more time at the office and less time with our spouse and children.

Finally, when you have trouble making decisions, it is always helpful to ask the advice of believers who know you well. They often have insights into your gifts that you lack and can be of great help in sifting through muddy waters.

Appreciate Perspective

Sitting by the pool with Yi-Wen, I asked her what her family was like. She is from Taiwan and is married to an American. Because of his U.S. government job, they have lived in several different countries and were living in our neighborhood for just a few months before going to

China. She and her husband came from such opposite backgrounds. Hers was Buddhist, his was Protestant. Not only were their customs different, but their expectations of family life were far from similar.

Here was I, raised in the south in a strong Christian family, marrying into another one as well. My husband and I came from similar educational and social backgrounds, and we have always lived in our native country. Yi-Wen and I couldn't have had more different experiences. In our brief time together, I learned from her. Her simple commitment to her husband impressed me. Hers has not been an easy life, and yet her desire to be supportive of her husband no matter what difficulties she encountered was an encouragement to me. Spending time with someone so unlike myself refreshed and challenged me, and it gave me a greater perspective through which to look at life.

Our natural tendency will be to spend time with people just like us. However, it is far more enriching for us and for our children to be with folks whose life experience has been different.

Have a believer from a foreign country to dinner with your family. Ask them to share about their life. Adopt a foreign exchange student for a semester. College towns have international students who would gladly welcome being "adopted" by a local family. Our vision for God's vast kingdom will be greatly enhanced by being with those from different lands.

Recently a friend phoned, concerned about her eight-year-old. They live in a wealthy community, and her daughter had begun to describe people according to the size of their houses. What really got to the mom, though, was when a baby-sitter told her that the child had been rude and remarked, "I don't have to pick up my toys, that's what my mommie pays you to do." Understandably, my friend was distraught. Both Mom and Dad thanked the sitter and proceeded to have a firm talk with their daughter. More importantly, these incidents made the parents realize that their children's values were being shaped almost exclusively by a wealthy neighborhood.

They began to seek out ways to develop family friends who did not have the same economic resources. In addition, they began to look for opportunities to care for and befriend those in need in the inner city. Social services have lists of needy families. Tremendous blessings can come when you spend time regularly with a needy family.

A two-parent family we know decided to reach out to a single-parent mom and her young child. This mom worked full-time and had many challenges raising her child alone. The other family invited her and her child to dinner on a regular basis, included them on several vacations, and stayed in contact by phone. Both families were enriched. One learned to be sensitive to the needs of those parenting alone, and another benefited from the advice and encouragement of a couple. And the children learned the importance of supporting one another.

Spending time with people older or younger than we are also broadens our perspective. My neighbor Edith is in her eighties. She has been such an encouragement to me, especially during the times I have felt overwhelmed by small children. A mother and grandmother herself, she appreciates my frustrations, yet because she is past her days of toddlers, she provides me with a refreshing perspective. When I think I'm a dreadful mother, she reminds me that I'm not and that this season will pass.

I suspect that when we are open to learning from people of different perspectives, our view of God will grow. We will be blessed by the vast ways He works in different lives, and we will be encouraged not to limit how He might choose to work in our own lives. Always allow God the privilege of working in another's life differently from the way He has in your own.

Our children can be taught at an early age to appreciate the benefits of perspective. Allison, at eighteen, comforts her eleven-year-old sisters when their fourteen- and sixteen-year-old brothers act awful. "Don't worry, girls," she says. "They are just teenagers, and it will pass. But for now, simply ignore them, and stay out of their way!" Ah, the wisdom of youth.

One mother comforting her teenage daughter who wasn't asked to a dance related her story of pain at being unpopular as a young girl. Through her mom's loving comfort the daughter realized that this wasn't the end of the world. Sometimes we just need a little perspective that whispers, "This will pass, and things will be all right."

Essential to appreciating perspective is reflecting on God's perspective. He is not limited by our views; He sees things in light of eternity. I find my own perspective restored when I consider the importance of my difficulty in light of eternity.

My problem just isn't that important when I think about it from the perspective of forever.

Hunger to Grow

My mother-in-law is an amazing woman. Approaching eighty-three, you would think that she would slow down just a little bit. However after a visit with her, I find that I am stimulated, refreshed, and exhausted!

She wants to know what good books I have read lately. What tapes have I listened to? What is God doing in my life? She shares about the people she is praying for, the woman she has just counseled on the phone, the letter she has just mailed. There's a new Bible study she wants to try and a young couple she wants to have over. She is concerned about a girl one of her grandsons is dating, and she is praying for another grandchild's college plans.

Vitality and spiritual depth are obvious to anyone she meets. What makes Grandmother like this? She has always had a hunger to grow. She wants to know more and more of the Lord. She desires to learn from others. And she never stops taking advantage of opportunities to develop her faith.

When I go in to kiss her in the evening, I often find her on her knees, white hair pulled neatly back in a bun, wrinkled, spotted hands folded tightly, and her lips whispering praises to God. In the morning, I peek in the door to find her propped up in bed reading her well-worn and much-marked Bible. Her desire to grow has a contagious element that affects those around her.

Her example causes me to ask, Do I want to grow? Is my passion in life to grow in my relationship with Christ and to help my children grow? Does this desire hang over all my decisions? Do my children see me reading God's Word, praying, taking advantage of teaching opportunities? What about our marriage? Are we seeking to grow deeper together? Do my children observe us taking time to grow as mates?

The way to develop our children's hunger to grow is to have a hunger in our own lives. But what if we don't have a desire to grow spiritually, in our marriage or in another way? Simply tell God. Ask Him to create within you a hunger. God wants our availability and will provide the means.

Spend time with a friend who is growing. Ask her to share what she is learning. Ask her to pray for you. We all go through dry times when it is encouraging to be with a friend who is excited about what she is learning. Her hunger can stimulate yours.

CULTIVATING TEACHABILITY

Valuing others, utilizing discernment, appreciating perspective, and maintaining a hunger to grow are four necessary components of a teachable spirit. In addition, there are several helpful things that we can do to cultivate this spirit in our lives and in the lives of our children.

Look for a Blessing

What is our attitude as we walk through life? We will face stimulating situations, boring assignments, embarrassing failures, and painful tragedies. If we have the attitude, "What can I learn from this situation or this person?" then we will grow.

Our own children get tired of hearing us say, "This is a growing experience." They think they've grown enough! Yet if we have the vision that God can use anything or anyone to draw us closer to Him, we will learn to look for His message, and we won't miss out on a potential blessing.

Our friend Logan, who has Lou Gehrig's disease, keeps telling us, "God is going to use my illness for good. He wants to teach each of us something special. He wants to use this in our church." Logan's attitude has instilled within those around him the vision that a tragic situation can bring a blessing.

When we look at life's challenges as opportunities to grow, and seek to learn something in every situation, *then* we won't miss out on a blessing.

Utilize Open Windows

From time to time in each of our lives there will be unique opportunities for growth. These "open windows" provide a chance to grow in unusual ways if we recognize and take advantage of them.

This past year I noticed that our sixteen-year-old son John seemed especially receptive to his dad. On the other hand, he appeared to think his mom was a bit silly. "Ah, Mom," seemed to be a common phrase around the house. Instead of despairing, we determined to take advantage of this "open window" in the relationship between father and son. Dad began to have breakfast out with John once a week before school. Over a quick meal, the "men" shared together. They studied the Word and often prayed. It has been a truly special time for their relationship.

Open windows come in the forms of relationships but also in the form of opportunities. A businessman in between jobs considers taking a three-week course at a seminary. He may not have this time available again for a long while. A single girl with no family responsibilities takes a month's leave from her job to go on a short-term mission project. An engineer who travels a lot contacts Christians in the various countries that he visits and is enriched as he sees the vastness of God's people.

Open windows are in front of us. When we notice them and take advantage of them we will be taught many blessings.

Expose Family to Vital Believers

Our son phoned the other night. He is spending the summer with other high school students as an intern at a wonderful Christian study center in New England.

"How's it going, John?" his dad asked.

"Fantastic, Dad. I've been reading some stuff by Francis Schaeffer, and he's awesome."

We had to laugh because sometime ago his dad had tried, with no luck, to get him to read that very book!

What was going on? Exposure to other believers, without Mom and Dad, was having a positive impact on our son.

One of the easiest ways that we can help our families cultivate teachable spirits is by exposing them to others whom we know will provide sound teaching.

A girl in our parish has an unusual volunteer job. She makes all the arrangements for visitors who want to come to our parish. Many are from other countries. She asks different people in our church to house them and spend time with them. Inevitably the host families are touched by the faith and diversity of those they entertain.

As parents, we have the job of thinking *exposure* for our children. Books, camps, and providing hospitality to individuals are just a few of the ways we can enrich our families and instill within them a teachable spirit.

A friend of ours loves to say that God is looking for F.A.T. people. A F.A.T person is Faithful, Available, and Teachable. I can't think of three better qualities to pray for myself and for my children.

FOCUS QUESTIONS

Meditate on Ephesians 4:1–32

1. What specific attitudes and concepts do you find here that will encourage the cultivation of a teachable spirit?

2. What attitude in your life do you need God to change? To develop?

3. What unique things do you learn from your spouse and your children?

4. List one special quality which each family member possesses that encourages you. Thank each person this week for one special thing he or she teaches you.

5. As you consider the ages and needs of your children, what is one action that will help you to cultivate a teachable spirit within each? (Remember: Look for a Blessing, Utilize Open Windows, and Expose Family to Vital Believers.)

Meditate on Psalm 25:4–15 and write a prayer sharing with God two things you would like Him to teach you. You might also make a request for each of your children.

*I will instruct you and teach you in the way
which you should go; I will counsel you with My eye upon you.
(Psalm 32:8)*

SELF-
DISCIPLINE
(John)

FOUR

*The chains of habit are too weak
to be felt until they are too strong to be broken.*

SAMUEL JOHNSON

*M*artin Luther described marriage as "the school for character." Nothing reveals the cracks in one's character more quickly than the strains of married life. But it is also true that, with the exception of the parent-child relationship, no other relationship has such potential to shape and mature character. In fact, family living demands every character trait which Susan and I are describing in this book, and especially the trait of self-discipline. I was reminded of this in a recent episode involving dear friends.

The voice on the other end of the telephone sounded desperate. I was deeply distressed because the young woman calling was the daughter of some of our oldest and dearest friends. Her new marriage had collapsed.

"John, it's been terrible," Sandy said. "So much of what I expected has just not happened. Charles [not their real names] seems too busy for me. He is obsessed with his job and surrounded by adoring younger people who think he is wonderful. He doesn't communicate with me; he doesn't understand why I want us to spend time together. He has hurt me so many times by what he has said; he seems to think I am different from the girl he fell in love with."

Things had become so painful that, after many tearful conversations with her parents and brothers, Sandy had left her husband and flown to be with family in the Midwest. Charles did not seem to care in the least. In fact, he even welcomed her absence. After a few days of separation, she had decided to call me. After all, I had counseled and married them. Perhaps I could offer some advice.

The situation was serious. However, these difficulties, while grave, were not insurmountable and were not so different from the challenges many young couples face sooner or later.

No one was urging this young couple to seek reconciliation. Everyone was upset; Sandy had been terribly hurt. Her friends couldn't bear the thought that she might be hurt even more before the process was over.

My advice to Sandy was not comforting.

"Get on a plane tomorrow and go back to him. Fight for this marriage with every ounce of strength you possess. Don't quit, no matter what Charles has done. You have too much going for the two of you to throw it all away. The one thing that must not happen is for you, ten years from now, to look back on this moment and wonder if you gave up too soon, wonder if you quit before you gave your very all to make this marriage work."

I suppose that it seemed like I was pouring gasoline on a burning house. I wasn't. I was trying to save a marriage and help two kids grow up.

Later, I finally tracked down the young husband and asked for his side of the story.

"John," he said, "it just hasn't worked out. She doesn't understand me or my needs. It must have been a huge mistake. Since the beginning we have had problems. What I want from her and what she wants from me are poles apart. It's been terrible. You just don't understand how I feel."

"No, I am sure I don't understand exactly how you feel, Charles. It sounds terribly hard. But, Charles, just think about this. *Immature men make decisions based on how they feel. Mature men make decisions based on what is right.* You know what is right, but you have to decide if you are going to keep on being a child and do what you feel, or if you are going to be a man and do what's right."

Here was a test of two young persons' characters. Pure and simple, were they going to *give up* or were they going to *grow up?* I was convinced that with God's help and with the help of some wise, patient counsel, this couple could grow through this time, could learn crucially important lessons, and move into a whole new depth of relationship.

Four or five months went by—no word at all from the family or Sandy. It was a bleak time, until early one morning I had a call. Charles

---

Immature men make decisions based on how they feel. Mature men make decisions based on what is right.

---

and Sandy were both on the line. I learned that with a broken heart but deep determination, Sandy had gone back to Charles to try again, and they were still together.

"John," *he* was doing the talking, not she, "we just wanted to call and thank you for the way you helped us last summer. You see . . . uh . . . we made it! We have been meeting with a minister, and he has greatly helped us. We're really happy. It's like we've got a whole new marriage now!"

I was too excited to remember anymore after that, except one thing Sandy said to me which I will never forget. "If we had to go through all that pain and anger and hell last summer in order for us to get to where we are now in our relationship, as awful as it was, I can honestly say I am thankful it all happened, and I'd go through it all again."

That's character, I thought. *That's maturity.* That conversation took place over a year ago. Since then, we have seen them and spoken with them and their parents many times. The turnaround has been nothing short of incredible. The growing up they have experienced and the mature way in which they are now helping other young couples is as encouraging as anything we have witnessed in twenty-five years of ministry.

They almost lost it, but in the end, Sandy wouldn't give up. She had character, and her character enabled her to discipline herself to do what she most feared and dreaded—to face the worst sort of pain and rejection with determination. She might have failed; after all, there were and are no guarantees—we have witnessed and reluctantly participated in the "funerals" of more than a few marriages. But even when just one partner has this sort of character, we have seen marriages reborn time and time again.

DEVELOPING SELF-DISCIPLINE IN CHILDREN

What does it take to help our children mature into people who choose the hard and difficult *right* over the easier but wrong way out? Caring parents will realize from the start that always to give their children what they want and to encourage the expectation of instant gratification is a huge mistake. Too, parents who always try to shield their children from pain and difficulty will ultimately harm them, because the child will never learn self-discipline and patience apart from working through difficulty and disappointment.

Surely as important as any aspect of mature Christian character is the trait of personal discipline. It is related to self-control—the ability to curb one's appetite or one's tongue, the ability to handle one's money wisely and turn away from temptation. Dependability is a facet—the ability to keep true to one's commitments and duty even when it is painful, inconvenient, and involves great sacrifice. Trustworthiness, responsibility, obedience to the law and to God, perseverance, stick-to-it-iveness, and determination are all part of self-discipline.

Some rare children seem to be born with discipline. One of our sons is like that. Even as a crawler in his crib he orderly arranged his toys. He has always been somewhat self-disciplined, responsible, and dutiful in an unusual way. Where does it come from? I don't know, but we all know not many are born with the discipline that one needs. There are areas in which we know we need to develop more self-discipline. Whether it is learning to control our tempers or manage our money better, it is the process of a lifetime.

Self-control is a Christ-like quality that is essential to personal happiness. The people we know whose lives are out of control are a disaster. Whether it is overeating, overcommitting, uncontrolled spending, a tongue that says what it shouldn't, a will that is weak, or working too hard for one's own good—lack of personal discipline usually leads to deep trouble. The fact that *disciple* and *discipline* come from the same root word implies that one cannot be a mature follower of Christ without the discipline to say yes and no as is pleasing to God.

Self-discipline and spontaneity are not mutual enemies. The self-controlled person need not be a bore or always predictable. A friend in college was great fun to be with because you could never predict how he would behave or respond. He had one crazy idea after another. He was

---

Self-control is a Christ-like quality that is essential to personal happiness.

---

the happiest guy I ever met, although sometimes I wanted to slip down through the floorboards when he pulled one of his crazy stunts. But he was good, and he was disciplined. It was said of William Wilberforce (the great nineteenth-century British abolitionist) that he was at the same time great fun and also moral. The self-disciplined person does not need to be a *prig*, but the person without self-discipline will usually prove to be a *pig*.

Most children are naturally undisciplined. Certainly as they grow older, life teaches them hard lessons about the necessity of discipline, but this may not be as true nowadays. When you combine a permissive philosophy of parenting with an increasingly materialistic society, you surely produce less disciplined, more self-indulgent adults. There is little doubt that this is true of our generation, and it may be getting worse.

When both parents work (or the single parent must work) and are therefore with their children fewer hours during the day, often they feel guilty. They worry that they are not giving their children all the love they ought. Therefore, they are less likely to discipline their children, and that produces undisciplined children who become undisciplined adults.

What is our goal in disciplining our children? First, my wife and I want to raise children who desire to obey God. A child who has not learned to obey his earthly parents will be unlikely to obey his heavenly Father. Second, we train our children in order to help them learn to manage their lives wisely on their own, so that they can one day become completely responsible for themselves.

Elsewhere we have written about the philosophy and procedure of disciplining children in the home, but we haven't tackled the question of how to develop self-discipline within the child, which is the other side of the coin.[1]

Here are seven practical suggestions for the development of self-discipline within our children.

1. Parents Present a United Front, Agreeing on What Is Right and What Is Wrong, What Is Acceptable and Unacceptable Behavior.

Children need clear direction, not one opinion from one parent and a different one from the other. In other words, kids need standards not stutters. If one parent demands the clothes be hung up at night and the other doesn't think it matters, what is the child to think? The child is going to be confused. If one parent thinks going to a PG-13 movie is okay and the other one doesn't, what's the child going to do? She will go to the one who says it's okay and precipitate an argument between the parents.

Jack was a bright seventeen-year-old and full of sexual appetite and anticipation. His mom expected him to control his urges and retain his virginity, but she did not discuss this with Jack. His dad was the public model of propriety but privately urged his son to "go for it" when he had the chance. You can bet whose guidance Jack chose to follow. I will never forget his telling me in detail about that night when he was finally able to indulge his appetites with a girl, over and over again. He later went home and told the whole story to his dad, who seemed overjoyed for his son. Promiscuity became a pattern in Jack's life—a pattern which years and marriages later he had never been able to break. A mixed-up message from his parents produced a mixed-up kid and a messed-up adult.

Wise parents will anticipate those areas in which their children are going to need moral guidance or guidance in any form of decision making. They will discuss the issue in advance and agree on what their expectations are so that they can present a united front to their child.

Are we going to let the kids drive in the car without buckling the seat belts? Are we going to tolerate it when they talk back? Are we going to make them go to Sunday school? Are we going to let them go out for the team or not? Is it okay to watch television on school nights or not? Is rudeness to one's sibling allowed to go unchallenged? When the rules of the house are disregarded, how are we going to respond? Are we unified in our commitment that our daughter needs to read a book for twenty minutes a day? If the child's grades are not what they ought to be, what is the remedy going to be? Do we punish a misbehavior one day and tolerate it another? Is this way of speaking acceptable in our home?

Parents have got to talk about these things and be united. But what if the parents do not share the same philosophy of parental discipline? What if one is too strict and the other overly lenient? A wise couple will realize this is a crucial issue and determine to do research in order to come up with a united plan. Visiting with an older couple whose children are mature, disciplined adults will be one valuable source of guidance. In addition, there are numerous good books available today that deal with the subject of discipline.

The bottom line is that we have a unified plan and that we communicate regularly as situations arise. Single parents particularly need to meet with other parents for advice and encouragement.[2]

2. Communicate Principles—Not Just Rules.

Jesus taught principles to live by, not rules to keep. The wise parent will do the same. Rules are important, but if we want our children to grow up knowing how to live the Christian life under constantly changing conditions, then we will work at instilling in them the unchanging principles that undergird Christian character.

It's not enough to say, "this is right, but that is wrong." That's fine for small children but is patronizing to children who are growing up. Communicating clear moral principles is one of the most crucial challenges in raising children, forcing us to reexamine our presuppositions.

Our two sons live in a very small bedroom. That's not their preference, but economic reality dictates that this be the case. Their twin sisters share a bedroom, too, that is only marginally larger. But the amazing thing to me is how neat those little girls are compared to the guys. So as you can imagine, one of the things we parents are constantly harping is "Guys, pick up your room—you have got to keep it neat."

One night one of the fellows asked, "Why?" Well, it caught me by surprise. I could have said, "Because God says so," but I couldn't think of a Bible verse to support my point.

I could have said, "Because I say so," and that is reason enough, but it struck me that perhaps since they are teenagers, they did need a few good reasons. So I gave it some thought, finally mentioning the following:

- Because you could trip in the dark
- Because your room has become a health hazard
- Because you can't find your own tennis shoes in this mess
- Because it is offensive to the rest of the family
- Because you need to learn how to keep your life in order

One step toward living an orderly and purposeful life is to bring one small portion of that life under control.

There were probably lots of other good reasons, too, but that was enough for one night. For a while it looked like my lecture made a difference, but eventually they fell back into the same old slime-and-grime routine. So I am trying another approach that for the time being seems to be working!

Whenever my mom punished me as a little child, she first would explain to me why she was doing what she was doing. This drove home principles of behavior rather than producing resentment within me, teaching me that there are good reasons for punishment and that discipline grows out of loving concern.

Let me quickly say, however, that a small child will not always be able to understand the why of discipline. There are times when it is enough to say, "Because I said so." As adults we are often faced with obeying God simply because He says so. It's hard and we don't understand, but when, as a tiny child, we have learned to obey our parents in this same manner, it will make it easier as adults to obey God.

When my son's report card was less than satisfactory, we instituted a mandatory study hall down in a little room in the basement. He squawked and complained and demanded to know why. A parent is not obligated to explain his or her reasons for taking certain actions, and I knew I didn't have to answer him, but I wanted to. He *needed* to understand why a quiet, orderly, systematic, and regular approach to study habits becomes crucial when one gets older. He pretended to be unhappy, but he and I both knew that the reasons were good and sensible. He finally said he guessed I was right, and it wasn't long before his grades went up again. This year his study habits are much more orderly—not because I am on his back about it, but because he realizes why this is important.

3. Be Strict When the Children Are Young—Loosen Up as They Get Older.

Many parents do just the opposite. They can't bear to raise their voice or lay their hand on their two-year-old. But when that kid has reached adolescence and is still behaving like a two-year-old, then they bring down the house on him. This does not make sense. The older the child becomes, the closer to adulthood, the more necessary it is for the child to decide for himself.

Little children need very clear instructions about what is acceptable and what is not. When they willfully disobey, they need to pay a price that will teach them to obey. People train small children in different ways; the punishment must not be more serious than the disobedience deserves. But if a little child is repeatedly allowed to misbehave at age three, then he will continue to misbehave at age thirteen, thirty, etc.

Watch parents of young children closely. Many seem to think that it is right only to *ask* their child to obey and then *ask* again. If the child remains willful and defiant, then they switch to tactic number two, distraction. They suggest some other activity as a means of changing behavior. If that doesn't work, they then either ignore the child's disobedience or begin to get angry and eventually overreact. The real problem here is that the child is in control instead of the parent.

The first five years, it seems to us, are the crucial years in which the building blocks of personal discipline are shaped. The battle, in most cases, is either won or lost then. If a child doesn't learn obedience at home, the teachers of that child in school have a very difficult problem.

Don't wait too long to begin to require obedience—a two-year-old understands plenty. Be clear about what is acceptable and what is not. Be clear about the consequences. Be consistent in discipline.

But a word of warning. We don't want our children growing up thinking that we don't love them unless they obey. A merit-based home is no fun, for kids or adults. Love and affection must abound no matter what. We want to build gracious homes, homes full of mercy.

I know a man who attended a boys' boarding school. A good school in many ways, it taught him valuable study habits, gave him the opportunity to excel, and helped him come into a whole new apprecia-tion of the honor system. The school was incredibly strict, but the young man noticed that many of the boys who finished and then went on to college immediately seemed to "go wild." They didn't study; they played all the time. They became very different people from what they had been in boarding school; the honor system was left behind. He pondered why this should have happened and came to two conclusions: (1) The faculty and staff too often stressed rules of behavior over reasons for rules. Had they emphasized obedience but underemphasized the un-derlying principles? (2) There was not enough loosening of restrictions as the students grew older. The eighteen-year-old had little more free-dom than a thirteen-year-old. Many parents make the same mistake. Continue to make your child's decisions for him, and when he leaves home, he will continue to let others decide for him—he will just go along with the crowd.

Teach good habits in the early years so that as your child grows he can begin to learn the underlying rationale. The simplest example of this is bladder control. You work and work to train this little guy how to do it himself! You think you are going to die if you have to take him to the potty one more time, but eventually he learns the trick and begins to keep it under control. The same principle applies to honesty, gossip, pouting, temper, and a host of other behaviors. You stay on them and stay on them until at last, they begin to get it under control. In the process, give them lots of praise and encouragement. They will then learn to praise others who struggle to learn new things.

When Susan was potty training the twins, she constantly praised them when they made it to the potty on time. Once when she herself went to the ladies' room, one of our toddlers followed her saying over and over, "Mommie, I so so proud of you!"

4. Give Your Child Responsibility.

The other night I did something that would have seemed very strange to most folks. I plopped both of our huge, thirty-gallon trash cans on my son's bunk before we left for a dinner party. It wasn't done in anger, and no harm was accomplished. I wanted to remind him of some-thing—his job is to take out the trash and then put the empty cans away. He almost always leaves the cans out front until I remind him to bring them in. He is not dumb. He has to walk within five feet of them when he comes in from school every day, so I know he sees them and doesn't forget. No, he is just a little preoccupied. So I decided that from now on, whenever he leaves them out unattended, I will put them in his

---

Giving your children jobs to do is one of the best ways to teach them self-respect, satisfaction, and a responsible self-discipline

---

room. Cruel? Stupid? Silly? No, I don't think so. Maybe a little crazy, but it is his responsibility, and we are determined that he learn to fulfill his responsibilities. Eventually, he will put the trash cans away.

Giving your children jobs to do is one of the best ways to teach them self-respect, satisfaction, and a responsible self-discipline. When the twins were four, I noticed that they were preparing their own lunches for nursery school. It unnerved me to see Libby climbing up on a stool to reach for the bread or the lettuce—she seemed so little. But then I noticed that they also seemed to get a kick out of it. Susan monitored what they prepared but let them do it. I asked her about it one day and her answer was so logical. She said you shouldn't do for a child what that child can do for herself. That demeans the child and discourages a proper sense of responsibility for herself. A child feels better about herself when she can tie her own shoes, choose her own outfit, and be counted on as grown up enough to take care of such things. Some parents coddle and baby their children and then wonder why the children are shy or afraid to go out on their own.

Generally, the principle is if the child can do it, then let him. Be clear about what the responsibility is, be positive about your confidence in his ability to do it, be appreciative and let him know how proud you are of his accomplishments, and stay on top of it. Be sure he learns to do it right.

Mowing the lawn has been the boys' responsibility for a long time. I pay them a little for it as a way to help them earn a bit of spending money, but not too much. They see it as a part of their responsibility to the family. I carefully trained them about the use and care of the mower, about safety procedures, and about what I expected in terms of weeding and trimming. If the weeding is not done, I see that they do it. But you can't be an ogre about it. You have got to stay on top of them with love and respect, letting them know how much you appreciate what they are doing, but at the same time that you want them to learn to "do it right." Once they have got it, then you need not inspect anymore, except in order to thank them for a job well done. Now the boys have started their own neighborhood lawn-care business. Learning to do their own lawn right gave them the confidence that they could do a good job in the neighborhood.

In such chores and duties, character is built. The child learns to glory in a job well done and learns to do his duty without complaining.

Don't be afraid to give your children responsibility. You will be surprised how much it helps them, not to mention how it helps you as well. In addition, it serves as great preparation for their own marriage and family life.

5. Appreciate the Value of Difficult Experiences.

There was a time when winning one's varsity letter in athletics was, at least for a boy, considered a great achievement which brought genuine respect and admiration from one's peers. Midway through my teen years, I transferred to a new school where I found a higher level of athletic abilities with a much greater challenge. Tennis had been my sport up until that time, but I couldn't compete with these fellows. So I began to experiment with some other sports. Halfway through the year, I stumbled on to a track and found that God had given me an ability to run. I didn't much like it but decided that you have to take what you have and do the best you can with it. It was run, run, run—in snow and ice, rain and broiling heat. Cross-country and the half-mile were my events, but a weak groin muscle was my downfall. I was the number two runner in the school and eventually in the state. But not until my senior year did the groin hold up through an entire season, enabling me to win my letter. At the year-end athletic banquet, my award was presented last, and the whole school cheered because I had finally attained my goal. My coach's words of praise and celebration that night carried me through some difficult times in the years that followed.

The hard, grueling work, the pain and disappointment and necessary perseverance taught me much more than I could have learned had I been a Cinderella star and achieved immediate success. I learned to push on even in great pain, to persevere rather than quit, to rejoice in the success of others, even when I was personally disappointed. I learned to wait and to wait, and that waiting really did not hurt me. I learned that one can be content even when he hasn't accomplished his goal and that, as Disraeli is reported to have said, "All things come to a man if he will just wait."

Learning to wait is a difficult task for our "instant everything" generation. We want success now; we desire a meaningful relationship now; we want it all—sooner than later. But life doesn't always go the way we want it. We have to learn, and we have to teach our children that we can't always have what we want when we want it. One blessing of difficult experiences can be that we learn the value of postponement. Perhaps we must postpone having that new car because we have unexpected medical bills. If, as a child, we learned to wait for a new bike, we will be better equipped to wait for the new car. If, as parents, we enable our children to satisfy their needs immediately, we will not train them in the art of waiting.

These qualities are essential but are usually learned not in the good times but rather in the difficult. Therefore, when your child wants to quit some endeavor that has not turned out as he thought it would or as fast as he wished it would, quitting may not always be the best solution. You may develop within your child the attitude or habit of quitting when the going gets tough. Think about it long and hard before you allow your son to quit his music lessons or your daughter her math homework. You are not just building a skill; you are also building character. Persistence, like strength, can be learned best in adversity.

Parents are sometimes afraid for their children to experience any pain, forgetting that Professor Pain teaches vital lessons.

When a young woman at whose marriage I had officiated left her husband a few years later, I spoke to her mother about the situation. It clearly had been a difficult experience for her daughter, who was now in the process of moving back home with her parents. When I asked about what efforts were being made toward reconciliation, the mother hesitated and then admitted, "I have been so worried about the pain my daughter has been going through, I haven't even considered that she might go back to him."

We must take care that we don't let momentary pain prevent us from making wise decisions with long-term ramifications.

6. Be Alert to Opportunities That Demonstrate the Need for Self-Discipline.

The world around us serves up almost daily examples of how counterproductive it is for individuals and for society in general to not exercise self-discipline. We can be aware of these and discuss them with our children so that they do not miss the significance of what is happening.

The whole nation has had to pay a huge financial price because a small group of bankers exercised what apparently was an unbridled lust for money. Uncontrolled anger leads to tragedy that often exerts an impact for generations. Uncontrolled lust for fame, success, sexual gratification, wealth, prominence, and a host of other temptations are repeatedly chronicled in the media. Call attention to this and talk about it so your children don't miss the obvious.

When the great baseball star Pete Rose was accused of and sentenced for repeatedly breaking the rules of major league baseball, it was apparent that the man had succumbed to an obsession for gambling. So disciplined and self-controlled on the baseball diamond, this incredible athlete had no control in another area of his life. A story like this will teach your children lessons they will not likely forget, but only if someone takes the time to sit and talk about it with them.

Our own lives as parents also provide ample opportunities for growth in self-discipline. In what areas are we negligent? Perhaps we have a tendency to use bad language or be overly critical of others. When we become aware of this and desire to change, we should ask our kids to pray for us. And when we slip, we ask them to gently remind us of our determination to be more self-controlled in our speech.

Drudgery can provide an excellent opportunity to grow in the virtue of self-discipline. Life is full of drudgery. A young mother facing an endless day of changing diapers, chasing toddlers, picking up toys, and finally falling into bed only to awake to the same tasks the next morning may feel overwhelmed by seeming drudgery.

An ophthalmologist may perform exciting eye surgery several times a week, but his major work of correcting simple refractions may bore him. No one is immune to boring tasks, yet how often do our children complain, "It's boring!" Immediately we feel guilty, and we wonder how we can make things exciting for them. We can't and we shouldn't. Self-discipline grows as we conquer a task even when it's boring.

7. Share with Your Children About Your Own Inner Struggles with Self-Discipline.

Kids generally think that adults, at least their parents, must have it all together if they correct and guide their children to develop self-discipline and responsibility. We do them a great disservice if by our silence we imply

---

*D*rudgery can provide an excellent opportunity to grow in the virtue of self-discipline. Life is full of drudgery.

---

that, "Well, once you're an adult this isn't a problem anymore." They need to know that one never reaches the point in life where he is just like a machine who always does the right thing.

When I was about fourteen, I recall vividly a day when my dad shared with me an extremely hard decision he had to make. I saw my dad in a new light. He was a human being just like me. Kids know this, of course, but tend to forget it.

Nearly every day we face hard situations in our lives. We have temptations to do things that we shouldn't or overlook or approve activities that are not right. We have challenges that we simply do not know how to handle some days. We fail. We have days when we feel lousy, when we don't want to be responsible or compassionate. I know this and you, the reader, know this, but do our children understand this aspect of being an adult?

Share some of your temptations and some of your failures with your son or daughter. Many things would be inappropriate to share with our children, but some are quite fitting. Perhaps you have a problem with speeding. Share this with your child, and ask him to pray for you and to help you be more disciplined. Am I way behind in some thank-you letters that need to be written? I know I need to be more disciplined in my letter writing. Simply by telling the children that I feel I am doing a lousy job in this area and asking them to hold me accountable for catching up by a certain date encourages me to get it done and helps them see that I too am still growing in learning self-discipline.

When we are willing to admit our weaknesses to our children, it shows we are human and helps them to realize that however old we are, we still live by grace. We all fail and must depend ultimately upon the mercy of God instead of our own virtue. Our children will come to have a more realistic understanding of adulthood, and each one will have a better grasp of himself and his own struggle. And in this process, his love for his parents will grow.

A wise man said that self-discipline is when your conscience tells you something and you don't talk back. Growing in that sort of self-discipline is a lifelong process. We don't suddenly achieve total self-control. At every stage in life, we have areas where we procrastinate and fail. But we do grow. If our children understand this concept and can see us growing, it will encourage them in their own growth. They will be as gracious in their own marriages and with their own children as we, their parents, have been. They'll laugh as they remember how we fussed at ourselves over our own failures, and they'll be encouraged to pursue without despair. The memory of an honest, growing parent is one of the best a child can have.

FOCUS QUESTIONS

Meditate on Luke 9:23

1. Can you remember a personal situation in which you made a very difficult decision to do what was right rather than take another way out? Now looking back, can you see any good that has come from your decision?

2. Is there an area in your life now in which you need to exert self-discipline? Is there someone you can discuss this with who

will pray for you? Plan a time when you will talk with him or her about this.

3. How do you rate yourself in the area of:

	Good	Weak	Needs Improvement
Self-Control: language			
temper			
money management			
appetite			
Dependability:			
Trustworthiness:			
Perseverance:			

- How would your spouse rate you? Your child?
- How are your children doing in each of these areas? What is one area to pray for and work on this week?

Meditate on Psalm 141:1–4, making it a personal prayer.

For God did not give us a spirit of timidity, but a spirit of power, of love and of self-discipline.
(2 Timothy 1:7, NIV)

COMPASSION

(John)

> *Teach me to feel another's woe,*
> *to hide the fault I see, That mercy I to others show,*
> *that mercy show to me.*
>
> ALEXANDER POPE

*I*t was one of those broiling hot summer days in Washington. I was running late. Hurrying in my unair-conditioned car, with a dark suit on that added to my warmth, I was on my way to a reception for a retiring staff member. Also waiting for me in my office was a young man from the Midwest whom I was to interview that afternoon. We had been looking for over a year for an assistant and felt that he might be the right person to join our staff. I was anxious to have a significant and thoughtful time with him.

So I was hurrying and a little frazzled—that might not be a bad description of my whole generation!

As I jumped out of the car in the church parking lot and headed toward the hall where the reception was in progress, out of nowhere a man materialized. Staggering up to me he said, "I can't get him up, I can't get him up."

He was shabbily clothed and smelled of alcohol. Like all city churches, we encounter lots of transients, some of whom are inebriated. I wasn't certain if this were the case, but clearly he was upset and panicked—his eyes were large with anxiety.

Glancing over to the bushes at the side of the lot, I saw a figure stretched out, motionless. There was no way I could tell from that one glance what his problem was, but I guessed that he had passed out from drinking too much on a hot morning.

67

I hardly even broke stride.

"I'll help. I'll get help right away," I said, and raced into the church, called the police department, gave a quick rundown, and finally hurried into the hall for the reception. Soon after that I met with the young clergyman, and the time went extremely well. In fact, he now is a member of our staff. But later on, when I finally slowed down enough to reflect a bit on the day, I remembered the man in the parking lot, his pleading eyes, and the immobile body in the bushes. I realized then that I didn't know what had happened to him. Worse, I hadn't called or even thought to ask someone else to inquire. In retrospect, I saw that I just had not cared.

Maybe calling the police was the right thing to do, and maybe the man was helped, but as I thought about it, I suddenly remembered the story of the good Samaritan. And all I could think was that I was like that priest in the story who just hurried on by the poor man on the road. I had been irritated that the fellow had interrupted me, rather than caring enough to determine how bad the problem really was, and I knew in my heart that, on that particular day, I had flunked the Compassion Exam. I just hadn't wanted to be bothered. Getting to meetings seemed more important than taking time for some fellow in the bushes. I was ashamed.

COMPASSION IS MORE THAN JUST CONCERN

Probably every person reading these lines has had similar experiences in which, only too late, did he realize that a person was hurting and he had pushed right by them, too busy to really notice. Sometimes it seems our whole society is flunking the Compassion Exam. Why is it? Is it because we don't believe in the importance of merciful acts? No, Mother Teresa is surely everyone's most-admired person. It's not that we don't think compassion is important, rather we somehow subconsciously think that our own agendas are just more important, and we pursue our own goals with such relentless energy that the needs of others are too often overlooked. It's not that we are not concerned for others, but our concern is too often not the same thing as compassion.

Are we really compassionate, caring people? Or are we guilty participants in a society that is in danger of developing a *hard heart?* What are we teaching our children about the importance of tenderly and passionately caring for other people in need? Are we modeling mercy or rather demonstrating a devotion to our own agenda that is subtly telling our children that what matters most is achieving one's own ends?

Much has been made of the growing need for volunteerism. We are noting "points of light" here and there as examples of how people are get-

---

It's not that we don't think compassion is important, rather we somehow subconsciously think that our own agendas are just more important, and we pursue our own goals with such relentless energy that the needs of others are too often overlooked.

---

ting involved in helping other people. We decry the excesses of the "me" and "greed" decade. But what we are seeing seems too often to be a temporary, secular, self-serving sort of altruism that is superficial at best. We don't see a lot of examples of people making great sacrifices on behalf of others. Rather than people "giving up" significantly, they speak of "giving back something" because "it really makes you feel good when you do."

My daughters have a Red Cross poster on their door that says, "Give blood—feel good about yourself." It's true—doing something good for another does make one feel better about oneself, but there is something significant going on here. Charitable groups hardly even use the word *sacrifice* in their pitch nowadays because it is not a popular concept.

A sociologist for Princeton surveyed two thousand volunteers recently as to why they volunteered. He divided the sample in half and asked the question in two different ways. The first group was asked: "If wanting to give of themselves" was an important reason people volunteered. Fifty percent said yes. But the other group was asked: "If sacrificing some of themselves was important." Only fifteen percent said yes.[1]

What people are saying is that they don't really want to be made uncomfortable or at least not for very long. We want to be caring and helpful to others *when it is convenient.* It is very difficult, for example, to get church members to take on long-term responsibilities. People will give a day or a brief time commitment to something but resist the request to make ongoing time sacrifices. We are too busy—or at least, this is what we say.

It is certainly possible to become so totally overcommitted to helping needy people as to have no life of our own, nor time to rest and be refreshed personally. Those experienced in the "helping" professions warn us of this danger. But most members of our generation are not inclined toward this error.

We know and believe that sacrifice, compassion, self-denial, and charity—qualities that blur and blend into one another—are essential to the Judeo-Christian faith that most of us espouse. Yet, we are often not as thoughtful and genuinely concerned toward others as we would like to think we are. The spirit of the age clearly is urging us to take care of ourselves.

CONCERN THAT ACTS

Compassion is having pity, feeling sympathy for another, and doing something about it. It's the opposite of envy at another's good fortune. The Greeks had a word for it that is worth noting—*splanchnizomai,* which means to be deeply moved in one's inner being by the suffering of others, to have one's heart significantly touched at the sight of crying human need. Early writers used this word over and over again to describe the reaction of Jesus to needy folk. When He viewed a large crowd of harassed and exhausted people, or a woman whose son had just died, or when two blind men blocked His way and begged His help, He had compassion. But it was more than sympathy or empathy. Rather, He was completely willing to use all means—time, strength, money—to come to the aid of another. Not just an attitude, compassion is action as well.

Jesus called it "mercy" and said in His Sermon on the Mount that indeed it is an essential quality for one who would be "happy." "Blessed are the merciful," He said, or "Happy and contented are the compassionate."[2]

Do we really believe this? Is the person who gets involved in the messy pain of another really going to find happiness? We tend to think that, *If I make a commitment to get involved with this need, it may cause me pain. I may end up making some major changes in my own life. I may end up feeling guilty about some things in my life and have to do something I don't want to do.*

These are legitimate questions, but rather than trying to assess these fears, consider a true story that illustrates the difference between just being concerned and having compassion.

One Heart Touches Another

I know a woman who developed a friendship with a high school girl in her neighborhood. Eventually the girl took an interest in spiritual things, decided she wanted to learn more about God, and suggested they have a Bible study. For a whole year this busy mother, with young children of her own, rose early on a weekday morning to meet before school with five teenage girls.

One of these girls came from a poor, underprivileged, and uneducated minority background. When the others talked about going off to college, this girl just assumed she would get a job at a fast-food restaurant and take it from there. No one in her family had ever been to college or apparently seriously contemplated the idea.

My friend, however, was not satisfied with this sort of acquiescence. Her heart had gone out to this young teenager, and she knew that somehow there had to be a way to help her go to college. They discussed it and prayed about it. It seemed a monumental task—no one had even dreamed this poor kid would ever go to college. Yet today, six years later, she has graduated from a fine college, and her first job out of school has been working in a home for the disadvantaged.

Yes, it took thought, prayer, work, determination, connections, late-night telephone calls, countless pep talks, but this girl made it because my friend who cared had *splanchnizomai!*

Where did this compassion come from? What made my friend different? What caused her to get involved even though she knew it might end up "costing her"? The answer lies within her *heart.*

At the heart of her character is an attitude of concern for others, a basic attitude God implants within each of us. We see it in little children in their natural sense of sympathy toward others. We call it tenderness of heart, sensitivity, generosity, or compassion. But most of us have grown up in a radically materialistic society that does very little to encourage the development of compassion. Rather we become *hardhearted.* Without our even realizing it, we tie tight cords around our hearts which constrict our sympathies. We commit ourselves to overly ambitious agendas, trying to do too much. We listen to the alluring advertisements which bombard us, and we tacitly accept the assumption that, of course, we have to have this and that product or gadget in order to have the basic necessities. Therefore, we accumulate too much. In an attempt to avoid stifling debt, we put off making significant financial commitments to our churches or important charities so that 99 percent of our money is diverted to our own bills and taxes and savings. This, too, tends to harden our hearts toward God's concerns.

We are trying so hard to experience all that life has to offer, but actually we are racing faster and faster in a circle around ourselves, with the result that God and others are on the outside, the periphery of our lives. Without even knowing it, we become hard-hearted. The hard heart becomes like a serious infection deep inside our body. We can't see it, but its infection seeps through the rest of the body and makes us sick. Until we get to the infection itself and clean it out, the whole body will suffer.

Restoring the Tender Heart

There are four concepts which have been helpful to many people in breaking through these hardened outer layers surrounding and isolating the heart. They are simple attitudes which, as we begin to adopt them, can genuinely help us to regain and recover the sort of tenderness at the core which God so clearly expects of us and which we ourselves want as well.

1. Understanding God's compassion. The first strategy for recovering a tender heart is to remember what God is like. A major reason compassion is becoming rarer in our day is that we forget that we, too, have been the recipients of great mercy. God has had compassion on us. Any person who seriously contemplates the holiness of God, the demands of His moral law as described in the Bible, realizes that none of us lives up to God's standards. And yet God has had mercy on us, He has taken pity on us, and forgiven us our sins. He's even gone further than that;

He has given us the gift of eternal life with Him in heaven. That's what we call *grace*. Mercy says, I pity you; grace says, I pardon you. Mercy looks favorably upon the negatives one does, while grace moves into the realm of taking positive action. Together these qualities comprise what we term a *compassionate heart.*

Suppose, just by way of example, you are stopped by a highway patrolman, having been clocked at eighty m.p.h. Now justice would say to you, "Here's your ticket, buddy." Mercy says, "I'm only going to give you a warning." But grace says, "Even though you are guilty, I am going to let you off. And I'll even buy you lunch if you are hungry."

That's mercy and grace and compassion all rolled up into one!

While the illustration is a bit farfetched, still it captures something of the giving, caring, compassionate nature of God. He has been compassionate, forgiving, and caring enough to give us much more than we deserve. We who have received God's mercy and grace then have the opportunity to be merciful, caring, and gracious toward others whom God loves just as much as He does us.

Many people have not understood or accepted God's gracious compassion toward themselves and so find it difficult to be compassionate toward others. Either they *assume* God just feels great about them and think little about it, or they are so burdened by personal guilt that they can't believe that God could love them and so continue to condemn themselves.

The message Jesus brought was that God is holy and righteous, His standard for us is perfection, but He loves us so that when we honestly admit how self-centered we are and ask His forgiveness, He not only forgives us but makes us His own children, taking us into His family. The person who has really come to understand this personally can never quite get over it and maintains a sense of overwhelming gratitude toward God. What God has done for us was absolutely unnecessary and simply done out of His love for us.

Felix Jardo, sixty, was a Philippine farmer who had been saving his money for years to buy a new ox for his farm. He finally saved the necessary amount and went out to look for the ox. He did not know, however, that the government had ordered all Philippine paper money to be exchanged for a new currency called the Bagong Lipunan. Therefore, his savings, stashed in the old currency, were useless.

So he sent a letter to the president of his country. He was only a poor ignorant rice farmer, he wrote, but he needed help. A reply was soon sent saying, "The law must be followed. Because the deadline for exchanging currency is already past, the Government can no longer exchange your bills with the new ones. Even the President of the Philippines is not exempt from this rule."

But the letter did not end there. It continued, "However, because I believe you really worked hard to save this money, I am changing them with the new ones from my own personal fund. I hope you will be able to buy your ox."[3]

The letter was signed by the president of the country. That unexpected and unnecessary sort of generosity is in some small way akin to God's compassion for us and His willingness to go out of His way to help us.

John Newton was a brilliant young Englishman who ran away from home and ended up a sailor at sea some 250 years ago. He soon lost what little Christianity he had received in his home growing up and became a self-seeking adventurer, bent on having as much fun and having as much money as he could. For many years he pursued the profitable slave trade and a profligate life-style, capturing Africans and transporting them to the Colonies. He spread his wild oats all up and down the African coast, and loved nothing better than to mock and undermine the faith of others whom he met in his travels. He almost lost his life once in a storm at sea, and this set him finally to reexamining his life and purpose. Eventually, he came to believe in Christ. He turned away from his former life-style and entered seminary.

Known all over England in his day, his turnaround was big news and kept him in the public eye. Overwhelmed by God's mercy toward him, he committed himself to working toward the abolition of the slave trade which had been his livelihood for so long. Slavery was eventually abolished by Parliament. Understanding God's compassion for him finally caused him to have compassion for others.

Newton later wrote the hymn "Amazing Grace," which has become a universally loved song exploring the compassion of God. He says in the song that for so long he had been *blind* to what was most important in life, but finally God had allowed him to see His amazing grace.

He once said as he reflected on this unexpected goodness of God,

When I get to heaven I shall see three wonders there. The first wonder will be to see many people there whom I did not expect to see; the second one will be to miss many people I did expect to see; and the third and greatest wonder of all will be to find myself there.[4]

This sense of *wonder* at the compassion of God causes one to look at others with the same sense of love and care. There are some very unlovable people in this world—murderers, child molesters, militant racists, and others. We find it very hard to view these people with compassion, but some of these same evils lurk deep within the heart of each of us. If God can have compassion on us, then He can forgive those sorts of folks as well, and we can become compassionate, too.

We necessarily will encounter spiteful folks, hurting folks, emotionally needy people, poor or injured people along life's way. When I remember that this sort of person is someone whom God knows and passionately cares about, I can be more compassionate as well. I may not understand their problem or approve of their life-style, but I accept them as important to God and important to me. Understanding God's mercy helps us to look at people differently.

2. It could be me. Related to this idea is a second concept: whatever need someone else has could be my own need, given a different set of circumstances.

A soldier loses a limb in the war and still suffers emotional and social trauma. That could have been me.

A girl gets pregnant in high school and drops out to have the baby. With no family support, she is unable to finish her education, and she lives in poverty. That could have been me.

A couple longs for a child, and after years of trying they finally conceive only to give birth to a retarded baby. That could have been my baby.

Had it not been for the "accident" of birth, I could have been that anxious man in the church parking lot that hot summer day.

There is no reason whatever to be smug about one's own accomplishments. God has given us the brains we have, and He enables us to have the opportunities that make it possible to enjoy whatever privileges and abilities we possess.

Instead, whenever we encounter a person who has needs, it does us a world of good to recall those words, *There but for the grace of God go I!* Sometimes this simple thought is all that is needed to release within us a flow of compassionate concern. You cannot solve everyone's problems and shouldn't try. But seeing people through this particular lens helps us to care. And sometimes there is a way we can help.

3. Righteous indignation. A third concept which helps us to become more caring about the needs of others is the simple idea of righteous indignation. "It's not right that this should be happening. We've got to do something."

How many of the privileges do we enjoy because somebody got good and mad somewhere along the line and did something about it? A fair day's wages, the right to disagree with my employer, equal access, equal opportunity, racial equality, freedom to worship are but a few examples.

Sometimes the simple unfairness of a situation galvanizes us to action, or it should. Not long ago we observed a situation like this in our town.

A young mother I'll call Sally had a long, discouraging day and was feeling a bit depressed. She decided to take a walk to lift her spirits. Instead of her usual path, she decided to turn in a different direction, which led her by the home of a single parent, Bea. Just as she approached Bea's house, Bea herself emerged from the door looking very distraught. As they talked walking down the street together, the story came out. A couple of years earlier, Bea had moved into a very old and extremely run-down house, one of the oldest in our community. As a hard-working single parent on a very tight budget, she had had difficulty making the kinds of changes in the home that she desired and were desperately needed. A frustrated neighbor had come to her angrily demanding to know when she was going to fix her house up because the way it looked "was a disgrace to the community."

It was nearly more than Bea could take. As Sally listened to the story, her own discouragements paled, and she knew she had to do something. There was just no way to sit back and do nothing.

Her compassionate nature, plus her visionary insight, began to go into operation as they talked, and a plan began to develop which she soon put into action. Through making a number of telephone calls and organizing a central committee, she was able to put together a team of people from her church and neighborhood who volunteered their time and money to come together on two massive workdays to scrape, paint, and do needed repair work on the house. It began to look like a different place. The new shrubbery in the yard, the lovely brass mailbox glistening, and the tasteful colors both outside and in, made a remarkable difference in the house's appearance. But the really remarkable thing was what it did, not just for the family that lived in the home, but for all the people who participated. A hundred people learned that with just a little vision, effort, and coordination, a family's life can be significantly changed.

A similar realization led to the establishment of what is known in Washington as "Christmas in April." Each April on a given Saturday hundreds of people work for the whole day down in the city to repair and renovate deteriorating homes in the inner city. It's infectious and grows each year. Often these tremendous things happen because someone got "fed up" and said, "We've got to do something."

4. *It could be Christ.* Finally, the realization that Christ Himself may be present challenges us to look again and to look with more compassion on others.

One of the most mysterious statements Jesus ever made was His comment, "Whoever welcomes one of these little children in my name welcomes me" (Mark 9:37, NIV). He spoke similarly on various occasions, implying that sometimes He will be in our midst and we will not recognize Him.

In the same way, there are instances in Scripture of God's angels coming among us as people in need and not being recognized. "Some people have entertained angels without knowing it. Remember those in prison as if you were their fellow prisoners and those who are mistreated as if you yourselves were suffering" (Hebrews 13:2–3, NIV).

Any person could be an emissary of God without our knowing it. Jesus Himself could be standing before us in the form of some ordinary person. The sheer magnitude of such a possibility causes us to see others in a different light.

The slow learner in your child's class, the elderly neighbor who rarely has visitors, the lonely teenager from a dysfunctional home, the overweight clerk who struggles to compute correct change—any one of these could be Christ Himself. This sobering realization can change one's entire perspective toward others and generate within us a sense of caring.

Understanding the heart of God, thinking "this could have been me," realizing how God works through righteous anger, and finally the incredible realization that sometimes the hurting ones who confront us might be God's very own emissaries—even Jesus Himself—these four ways of thinking can enable us to become more compassionate people. The hard heart can begin to become tender once more.

But what about our children? How can we protect them against the hard-heart syndrome?

WHAT OUR CHILDREN OBSERVE

The example we set for our children will help them, perhaps more than anything else, to grow up into compassionate men and women. This begins, of course, with the spirit of compassion right in the home. I can remember being carried by my mother on visits over and over again as a little boy—various errands of mercy among the poor and the sick of our small Southern community. She always seemed to be thinking about them and the needs and concerns they might have. Sometimes it was simply visiting or taking a loaf of bread or a pound cake to someone, or loaning some of our nice things to a poor woman so that she could "dress up" her house when she was having a party. It may have been sitting with the hairdresser whose husband was dying of cancer. Always it was a time to encourage them and to pray for them.

Dad was a hardworking and successful businessman who also loved God. I can still hear him telling us stories of needy folks he would run into and the joy it brought him to help them out. "Son" he used to say, "you can never out-give God." He was full of compassion.

Kids see this kind of *care* and imbibe it. They drink it in, and it becomes a part of their being. But if they see their parents focused solely on the job or the home or the church or whatever, resenting those times when needy folk intrude into their lives as bothersome interruptions, then they will likely grow up self-focused and calloused to human need.

It is wise to ask ourselves, "What sort of picture am I giving my children of how we are to respond to needy, hurting people?"

The brother of a friend of ours had AIDS. As his condition worsened, Sue realized she had to go and be with her brother, who was then living in San Francisco. For several months, she lived with him and cared for him, but as he continued to deteriorate, Sue began to feel that she wanted to bring him home to spend his last few months with her own family. However, many questions raced through her mind: *What would her friends think? How would their neighbors respond? What about the Christian school where she was the director? How would the staff and students' families respond? And what about the risks for her and her own husband and children?*

The risks to her family were frightening, and the demand it would make on them would be enormous, but her husband agreed it was the only thing to do. He said, "Sue there are some things more important than life, and this is one of them."

There was really no question in the end.

Sue, John, and the boys took care of him, shared his pain and suffering, and wrestled with this awful disease. They all learned more than they had ever known about what it means to be a family, to be loyal, to care. They helped him come to a strong faith, saw him baptized in his bedroom by a minister from our church, and stayed beside him when he died.

For most of us that would have been the end. They had showed compassion to a remarkable degree, and God had blessed and protected them. But that wasn't the end.

Recently, they have organized a committee in the church to care for other HIV+ people, and now have another young man with the same disease living with them. A group of people with AIDS and their friends meet regularly in their home now to share, to study the Bible, to encourage one another, and to pray. The parents are teaching compassion to their two sons by the way they live.

This needn't just occur in such dramatic situations. Not many of us will find ourselves in a dilemma like this family. But often we do have opportunities to demonstrate compassion in the daily, commonplace activities of life, and our children are often there to observe, to remember.

Turning Toward Suffering

The other night around eleven o'clock the telephone rang. That's pretty late for me, particularly at the end of a long Sunday. When I heard the voice on the other end, I was surprised. It was a man I had known twenty-five years ago in college but had barely seen or heard from since. He was at National Airport and in trouble. The last thing I wanted was someone in trouble, especially at my bedtime! But there are times when compassion has to overrule convenience. I could have been the one at the airport in trouble. Or it could have been my son.

His story was almost beyond belief. Toby had some slight problem in his earlier years with skin cancer but nothing dreadfully serious. Two or three months before this call, however, he had banged the back of his neck against a car door, and a tiny mole had suddenly erupted into violent life. It was cancerous. It had grown rapidly to the size of a grapefruit and now had spread cancer to other parts of his body. Toby had been the recipient of some poor medical care that had actually aggravated rather than reduced the growth. After much study and many consultations, he had flown to Greece to receive treatment from a controversial physician who had remarkable success with an experimental drug not approved in our own country. Toby had made the trip safely and had just commenced treatment when the doctor suddenly died, leaving no one to carry on the work. His last hope now shattered, Toby was stuck at the airport, sick, lonely, and afraid. He needed a place to stay and someone who cared.

That was the first of several late nights and busy days with Toby as we tried to help. The cancer had in some ways marred his appearance, and it was painful to be with him, but what an opportunity it was for the whole family to be close to someone in great pain and need, to listen to him, to learn from him what it is like to battle such a deadly opponent. We became more sensitive to the pain and fear of others. And we realized that someone whose appearance is sometimes difficult to stomach is just the same as the rest of us inside.

In a way, cancer became more bearable to us as we observed Toby's ability to laugh and joke in spite of the seriousness of his situation. We learned some valuable lessons about how not to respond to cancer as he told us of some of his mistakes. But even more important, Toby's faith and peace were so great that we saw in him how a person of faith responds to such a frightening disease. We realized that God gives you the ability to trust Him, to depend upon Him, and even to have joy right in the very face of death.

Our children were deeply touched and moved by having Toby with us and will always see cancer patients in a different light from now on. Now that Toby has been with us, we have some idea what it is like for a person sick with cancer.

We live in such an antiseptic age that we are often walled off from needy, hurting people. This ignorance breeds fear and causes us to turn *away* rather than turn *toward* hurting folk.

But when we turn toward them, compassion grows, and we are all enriched.

Imagining What It Is Like

Relationships like this help my wife and me and our children immeasurably because they enhance our ability to know or imagine what it must be like to be in need. If we can imagine what it is like to be in someone else's situation, then we can better understand and help them. We *want* to.

Several years ago, a book entitled *The One-Minute Manager* sold thousands of copies. The thesis was that simply by taking very brief moments of time interacting with employees, a manager could make major contributions to the effectiveness of the employee's work and could also raise staff morale and the sense of organized teamwork.

In much the same way, one can make good use of just one minute in the right situation for "one-minute imagining."

As we encounter a person with problems, in only a brief amount of time we can give that person our total attention, listen carefully, hear what they are saying, and observe through their expressions and body language a great deal of what they are feeling. We can consciously put ourselves into their situations, imagine what it must be like, and often find that our hearts respond with compassion as our heads thoughtfully take in what we are hearing and seeing. We can teach our children to do this as well.

Once several years ago, I watched with fascination as a blind man disembarked from the subway, rode the escalator up to the street, felt his way across the intersection, and walked up the street. I was sensitive because my own eyesight was rapidly deteriorating, and I had been warned I might lose my sight as well. As I watched, I imagined what it must be like, and that night told the children about it. We even went so far as to walk around the house with our eyes closed to try and get some sense of what it would mean not to be able to see.

Not long after that my own eyes began to deteriorate much more rapidly, and soon I was able to see almost nothing out of one eye. I had a corneal disease for which there was no known cure. But before I lost the sight in my second eye as well, I was able to undergo a corneal transplant and regain my vision. A year later I had a surgery on my other eye and then eventually had surgery again before my sight was thankfully, fully restored in both eyes.

When our church congregation first learned of the seriousness of my problem, one man came to me and told me he had two good eyes and he wanted to give me one of them. It was not feasible for a number of reasons, but his compassion to me then is still overwhelming to me and my family even now, ten years later. My family and friends suffered through that time with me and now have a better understanding of what blindness is like. Therefore, we can all be more practically helpful to persons with eyesight problems.

Teaching our children to use their imagination to feel and think what it must be like to be a victim of a tragedy or to have any kind of need is surely one of the best ways to engender genuine compassion. We can make great use of the television to help us if we are alert to situations in the news or shows that make us more aware of the needs of others and will take the time to share with our children our thoughts and feelings about these things.

Being alert to people who are hurting can often make a big difference if we will grasp some of the opportunities. We are surrounded everyday by wounded people—persons who have become physically or socially or emotionally debilitated. There is certainly in your life a person like the wounded man on the roadside in Jesus' story of the good Samaritan. You may see that person as a burden or as an obstacle to your own pleasure, but the truth may be that person is there because God put him there so that you can give away what God has given to you. The wounded of the world are there for us. God will show us how we can best serve them if we are willing to be a neighbor. The result? We will begin to live life to its fullest.

WHEN COMPASSION BACKFIRES

Showing compassion doesn't always lead to a happy ending. A friend of mine has what I consider to be an unusual love for animals. She is always drawn to them and they to her. One day she was alarmed to hear the most frightening choking sounds coming from the neighbors' backyard where their dog was chained. Since the neighbors are invariably away from home all day, she went into the yard to investigate. She found to her horror that the dog, who had been left attached to a strong line, had become so entangled that he was hanging by the neck with two feet barely touching the ground. He was close to choking to death. Rushing into the yard, she struggled with the chain and finally had to cut it in order to free the dog. She took the badly frightened dog into her home and telephoned the owner at work.

To her utter amazement, the neighbor, rather than expressing concern for the animal or gratitude, was irate that she had trespassed and

---

Teaching our children to use their imagination to feel and think what it must be like to be a victim of a tragedy or to have any kind of need is surely one of the best ways to engender genuine compassion.

---

interfered. In crude language, the man made it clear that he did not believe my friend and stated in no uncertain terms that she should not have butted in and should never do so again. To say my friend was taken aback was an understatement.

Getting involved when others are hurting isn't always safe. It's not unusual to get hurt when you try to help. A needy person may also be a dangerous person. A hurting person may hurt you. A messy situation may involve you in ways that are difficult, painful, dangerous, even disastrous.

This tragic sort of thing we all fear. We dread that somehow our getting involved may backfire, and we may get hurt ourselves. It's so much easier to turn away and so much safer. But if we all turn away, an even worse thing will happen. The poor will become poorer, the sick will die, the hurting will multiply, but worst of all, our hearts will begin to shrivel up and become hardened and insensitive. God can do great things through a teachable, risk-taking, compassionate person. But He can do precious little with a hard heart. None of us can solve all the world's problems. There are needy situations we'll encounter that we can do little or nothing about. But a compassionate person will do what he can. Our reward isn't necessarily getting strokes here on earth for all the thoughtful good we have done. Sometimes exactly the opposite will happen, and we'll regret, perhaps, even getting involved. But we take the risk anyway because we know it's what God would have us do.

This is at the very heart and core of what it means to be a person of strong moral character.

When I was a boy, we used to see advertisements to give to the refugees and needy folk overseas. The symbol of the organization was a box, presumably containing much needed goods or supplies, with the large letters C.A.R.E. stenciled on the side. As I've reflected on that symbol for nearly forty years since first seeing it, I've come to the conclusion that C.A.R.E. may be the most important word we ever learn. It is the very heart of Christian living.

FOCUS QUESTIONS

Meditate on Isaiah 58

1. Isaiah the prophet observed that the people of his day would periodically do something "religious" (in this case fasting), but that they really did not demonstrate a spirit of compassion toward others. Is there some parallel in your life that God wants you to consider?

2. Are you a compassionate person? What would your spouse say? your neighbor? your child? Is there a particular person or situation in which you know you should be more compassionate? Which of the four strategies in this chapter would be helpful for you to consider?

Meditate on Psalm 103:1–18, thanking God for the ways He has shown compassion to you.

I, even I, am the one
who wipes out your transgressions
for My own sake; and I will not remember your sins.
(Isaiah 43:25)

A SERVANT'S HEART
(Susan)

It is high time the ideal of success
should be replaced by the ideal of service.

ALBERT EINSTEIN

*W*e had agreed to meet at the entrance to the park for our early morning walk together. The chill of winter's last embrace was already causing my breath to "smoke" and my toes to freeze as I waited impatiently for my friend Aimee to arrive.

This was a day to go back to bed, not be an exercise fanatic, I groaned as I stomped my feet to keep warm. I wished I hadn't come. I was already in a foul mood, and my day ahead was going to be anything but pleasant. The house was filthy, and I had to host a meeting in it tonight. Three of the kids had dental appointments, and I hadn't balanced the checkbook in two months. An uncompleted magazine article was still on my desk, past due. Plus, a friend whose feelings I had hurt was coming to talk to me. And my husband had left for work frustrated with me because I asked *him* to pick up a couple of things for me on his way home tonight. After all, I had to cart five kids all over town today and do other mundane chores which no one would appreciate.

Aimee's cheery greeting interrupted my self-pity party, and we began to walk rapidly along the winding path. Sensing my gloomy mood, Aimee became quiet as we walked in companionable silence. Her sensitivity never ceased to amaze me. In fact, her attitude toward life constantly surprised me.

A few years older than I, she was on her second marriage. Her husband was not a believer. Between them they had several troubled teenagers. One was gay, another on drugs, another living with different girls, and that was only the beginning. Her mother-in-law lived nearby and was a miserable person who constantly took out her frustrations on my friend. Her husband was often unpleasant, largely ignored her, and was completely lacking in affection or tenderness. Aimee was new in her love for the Lord, and yet she had learned the secret of experiencing joy despite her circumstances.

A few days earlier she had remarked, "Yesterday I woke up in such a bad mood. I really began to feel sorry for myself. Then as I realized what I was doing, I knew it wasn't right. So I said to myself, *There are plenty of people in worse situations than I am. What I need is to do something for someone else.*"

So she washed and brushed her small dog, put bows on him, got in the car, and drove to a nursing home (where she knew no one) to visit elderly, ill patients. The joy she felt was only surpassed by the joy which she and her dog gave to the lonely patients.

Aimee has learned the secret of a *servant's heart*. Instead of focusing on herself,·she continually seeks to reach out and care for someone else. I have seen her do this in many different ways, usually not a big deal but always an act of kindness: a meal for a tired young mother, a note of encouragement, a quick phone call just to say, "I'm thinking about you."

Certainly Aimee has a real right to be miserable. And yet she isn't. She is joyful. Her attitude both convicts and encourages me.

By her example, she challenges me to cultivate a heart that seeks to serve others.

Why is Aimee so unusual? Why is she joyful? The answer is so painfully obvious and so very simple, and yet so hard to do. Cultivating a servant's heart is a tremendous challenge for today's families. Why?

The fast-paced society in which we live exerts many pressures. There is great *financial pressure*. Affordable housing is difficult to find. Food, utilities, clothing, and transportation costs have risen substantially, and many are faced with considerable college tuition bills. There are more gadgets to acquire which create more repair bills. There are too many good opportunities to take advantage of—all of which seem to cost money.

There is also *coping pressure*. Single parents are trying to cope with the challenges of their children's needs. Families are coping with ill and aging parents and young, demanding toddlers at the same time. Many are coping with the effects of their own dysfunctional childhoods. Counselors are overwhelmed with people seeking help simply to cope.

Added to this is the tremendous *success pressure*. A loud message screams at us that personal value is measured by success—success on the

---

Self-concern is not in itself wrong, but our self-focus is in danger of becoming so vast that the capacity to care for others is eroding.

---

football field, in the classroom, at the law firm, in parenting. Failure is shunned, and significance has become the new "god."

As parents we face overwhelming pressures, and our children often mirror these pressures. One nursery school teacher compared her three-year-olds of today to her students of ten years ago. Today's three-year-olds appeared to be more independent.

They entered the classroom and headed straight for the toys. They appeared more grown up, more self-assured. They seemed to communicate that they were in charge. But as she watched, she also noticed that today's three-year-olds were less generous, less courteous, and had very little thoughtful concern for others.

Instead, they were more hurried and more self-seeking.

These pressures on our families unconsciously force a *self-concern* upon us that is not particularly healthy. We are worried about how we are going to get by, how we will make it.

Life seems to throw us back upon ourselves, and the result is that we think more about ourselves—job security, financial needs, obligations, even our families—than is healthy.

Self-concern is not in itself wrong, but our self-focus is in danger of becoming so vast that the capacity to care for others is eroding.

When the pressures of this world are combined with our own self-serving nature, we are headed for trouble. Because of our sin nature, our natural tendencies will be either to *satisfy* self, to *serve* self, or to *feel sorry* for self.

Yet Christ has called us to *deny* ourselves.

The uniqueness of Christianity is a deep genuine concern for others. What, then, is a *servant's heart?*

One with a servant's heart is one who genuinely seeks "to love his neighbor as himself," that is, to see ourselves as responsible for the care of others. We are not our own, rather we belong to God, and His desire is for us to actively, thoughtfully, graciously care for others—wherever we find ourselves and in whatever we are doing.

Life in the nineties thrusts us upon ourselves. Christ points us to others. At the heart of how we view life and how our children will see life is either a concern for self-fulfillment or a commitment to serve others.

The danger for us as parents is that we will unintentionally produce a generation that no longer has a servant's heart, but instead one whose overwhelming goal is to look out for themselves—number one. Today's rule, "Use others to get what you need," is becoming a standard, replacing the Golden Rule, "Do unto others as you would have them do unto you."

Our challenge is to halt the trend and recapture Christ's call to love others as He has loved us—sacrificially—as a servant.

A servant's heart is not natural. It must be cultivated, and this begins in the family. I have to realize that I must work at this trait. It will not just happen in my own life nor in the lives of my children. The great thing about growing in character is that I can't do to my kids what I am unwilling to have done in my own life. As with the other traits, I must seek not only to train my children but also to grow myself.

THREE TRAPS TO AVOID

Before considering how to cultivate a servant's heart, it is helpful to recognize three common traps which snare each of us.

Often when we are faced with the opportunity to help someone these subtle questions pop into our minds: *Is it convenient? Will it benefit me? Do I feel like it?*

Is It Convenient?

In our hectic lives most people's needs will infringe on our time. Our fifth grader needs help with her math just when my husband and I want to read the paper. A neighbor asks for a ride to the airport in the middle of the important game on TV. A business associate calls to talk about a personal problem right when we are about to finish an important report. People just don't seem to pick times that are convenient to us when they need help.

Will It Benefit Me?

Is there a financial gain in this act of service for me? What about credit? Are there risks? Will my participation look good on my resume or to my friends? Will I gain public recognition? What are *my* returns?

We live in a city famous for public servants. There is a certain glamour about this sort of servanthood, but the servanthood which Jesus calls us to is not glamorous, not one "photo op" after another.

Do I Feel Like It?

I don't feel like helping my mate with this project; after all, it's his responsibility. I don't feel like helping him with this situation; after all, he got himself into this mess. I don't feel like that's my job; someone else can do the dirty work.

Sometimes these questions are valid. But when we are honest with ourselves, we will notice that more often than not we use them selfishly as barometers to determine if we should serve our fellow man.

Jesus has called us to lay down our life for our friends (John 15:13). Yet often I find it difficult to simply lay aside my own desires for my family and friends.

FIVE INGREDIENTS FOR A SERVANT'S HEART

What, then, are several qualities which will enable us to cultivate a servant's heart in our own lives and in the character of our children? Five ingredients make up the recipe for cultivating a servant's heart.

1. Kindness

A friend who recently went back to teaching in a public junior high school told me that her greatest adjustment was in dealing with kids who were cruel to one another. Another friend who teaches nine- and ten-year-olds in a Christian school says that her most difficult challenge has been the nasty way her female students treat each other.

In my own marriage, I sometimes find that I am unconsciously kind to my husband only when he has expressed tangible kindness to me. It's as if I keep a credit report. If he's nice, I'll be nice. If he isn't, I won't. How far from God's way this is.

If we are truly honest with ourselves, we will know that we all have a long way to go in growing in kindness. How can I begin to grow in kindness myself, and how might I help my children cultivate this as well?

Kindness will be observed most clearly in speech and in actions.

Kindness in Speech. "Sticks and stones might break my bones but words will *always* hurt me." We all learned a very different jingle, but the truth is that our tongue can be used to encourage or to wound. Proverbs 15:1, 4 states, "A gentle answer turns away wrath. . . . A soothing tongue is a tree of life."

"You dummy," "You're stupid," and "Oh shut up" are exclamations you might hear in a typical home of young children. While this is an exhausting time for the frustrated parents, it is also a crucial time for teaching the small child to be kind to his siblings.

We found it helpful to explain to our children that these words were unkind and were not permitted in our home. You could disagree with one another, but you could not be rude or say unkind things about a person. When these words came out, we washed the offensive mouth out with a little soap. It did not take long to make the point.

Learning to praise is a positive means of teaching kindness in speech. As our children learn to say "please" and "thank you," we should praise them. In turn, we can help them speak kindly to one another. Reminding a four-year-old to say, "You have colored a very good picture," to his two-year-old sister builds the habit of using kind words.

The same standard in speech applies to us as parents. I cannot require that my children speak kindly and then speak cruelly myself. I remember getting into trouble when I was young over something I said. At the time, what I said did not seem hurtful to me. My parents however explained, "Susan, it's not *what* you said, it's *how* you said it." My speech reflected sarcasm, a put-down, or was said in a way that communicated that I thought the other person was stupid. Not very kind. I'm still learning that my tone or manner can be just as harmful as my actual words.

It's difficult to take back unkind words, but we can ask forgiveness when we say things we shouldn't. And we can begin to think before we speak.

Kindness in Actions. Recently my car wouldn't start. I had just loaded groceries into the trunk and was sitting in the parking lot of the grocery store unable to move. The bag man noticed my trouble and walked over to offer his help. Of Asian descent, his command of my language was minimal, and I did not know his. However, he took a couple of minutes to help me locate the problem and start the car. *How kind he is,* I reflected. As I was about to leave, an angry customer ran up to him and proceeded to cuss him out for his delay in retrieving her bags. *What a contrast in character,* I thought sadly.

There is indeed much rudeness in the world, and in many places it has become the norm. Drive in city traffic and you will wonder what has happened to kindness. If we want to recapture acts of kindness, we will have to create specific opportunities for ourselves and our children to show kindness.

Meet a new mother at the bus stop. Invite her for a cup of coffee and introduce her to others in the neighborhood. Offer to do some office work that is not normally yours for an overwhelmed co-worker. Mow a neighbor's lawn who is out of town. Make cookies for a college student in exams. There are many opportunities to be kind if we simply look around us.

Our twins have begun to baby-sit. When they first began, we had our familiar chat with them about cleaning up. When each of our kids baby-sit, I expect them to clean up the house where they are sitting. Dishes must be washed and toys put away. Even if the mess was there when they arrived, I still want them to clean up. Most likely there is a tired parent who is coming in late and would greatly appreciate arriving at a clean house. I know! I used to be a tired parent, and coming home to a house left a mess by a baby-sitter was most discouraging. More importantly, though, is the lesson I want my kids to learn—*be thoughtful of others.* These parents are tired, so be kind and clean up for them. Instilling a thoughtful spirit in my kids is the issue, and baby-sitting simply provides one opportunity for building this trait.

It's easier to be kind in our speech and actions with those we like, because we want them to like us back. But what about those we don't especially care about? That's harder for parents and children, but that's where genuine virtue is exhibited. Is there a lonely adult in our neighborhood who would appreciate being invited to a family meal? How about at the office? Is there someone that is left out when the usual crowd goes to lunch?

A question we often ask our kids is, "Are there any lonely kids in your class? Who is the child that no one wants to play with on the playground, that no one asks to join them for lunch? What can you do to help this child?"

At our school, we have parent-teacher conferences in the lower grades. These conferences provide a wonderful opportunity for parents to let the teacher know that character is important to them. We tell the teacher that we want our child to be kind and respectful in his speech and actions with them and with their fellow students. We would appreciate their reenforcing this. We ask the teachers how our child is behaving in his or her treatment of other children. Is he kind? Does he reach out, or does he leave others out? A couple of years ago, a teacher told us that our twins were leaving others out. We had to deal with this, and it took several months and several talks with the teacher. But it was a wonderful hands-on opportunity for our girls to grow in kindness.

Academics are important, but character building is more important. Teachers can be of tremendous help to parents, but parents must let teachers know that character is important to them.

At the end of each year, we check in again with the teacher to see if there are things we need to work on over the summer. You'd be surprised how it encourages teachers to know that parents are interested in building character.

School provides a laboratory for developing kindness but so does the family, and chores can be a positive tool in this process.

In most families the days of full-time help are over, and often both Mom and Dad work outside the home. However, there are still meals to be fixed, dishes to be done, the house to be cleaned, and so on. A family where each member does his or her part will be a family that is learning to be thoughtful by providing needed help.

In our family of seven, we have a daily dish chart. Two different people pair up each evening to do dishes. On weekends, we divide the house into seven sections. Bathrooms must be cleaned, and each room needs dusting, vacuuming, mopping, and so on. Chores rotate, and everyone helps. Of course, chores aren't greeted with enthusiasm, but when small children are given appropriate tasks, they quickly learn that this is simply part of family living. Everyone must help. Having a list

---

*A*cademics are important, but character building is more important. Teachers can be of tremendous help to parents, but parents must let teachers know that character is important to them.

---

drawn up ahead of time and posted on the refrigerator alleviates much of the natural whining. Family members may trade with each other when they both agree.

Chores provide benefits as well. A child's self-image grows when she realizes she can make a contribution—no matter how small—to family life. Relationships between family members are developed when we work together with someone else. And our children learn good habits for their own marriages and families in the future. A chore well done gives us an opportunity for appreciation as we thank our child for his good job.

2. Appreciation

Closely related to kindness is appreciation. It seems so obvious, and yet our society is malnourished by a lack of appreciation. Often in the family, where it should be the greatest, it is most lacking. Our natural tendency is to take for granted rather than to appreciate. Your four-year-old is not likely to say, "Boy, Mom, you're doing a great job of raising me." It is an unusual husband who will comment, "Sweetie, I appreciate your carpooling the kids all over the place today," or a wife who remarks, "Honey, I appreciate your going into the office even when you don't feel like it."

It is helpful to think of appreciation in two areas: appreciation for *who* you are and for *what* you do.

Chris and John both made the varsity tennis team this year. As the youngest on the team, Chris didn't get to play very much. After one of their matches in which he did not play, I gave him a hug and said, "Chris, I'm so proud of you."

"Why, Mom? I didn't even play," he responded.

"Because you're my son, and I'm proud to be your mom," I replied. We appreciate and support each other simply because we are family.

We have a favorite version of "spin the bottle."

We sit in a circle to play this game. When the spinner lands the bottle, she tells the person to whom it is pointed something that she appreciates about him or her. Libby once appreciated Allison because she let her sleep with her occasionally and didn't get too mad if she wet the bed. Chris appreciates John because he helps him on the computer. Sometimes, in a family prayer time, we simply take turns thanking God for something we appreciate about the person sitting to our right.

A couple of years ago, I led our senior high school's student council retreat. In talking over the plans for my session, I asked my kids what they thought of playing the "spin the bottle" game with the students and faculty divided into small groups. Now, ours is a public high school with a variety of faiths, races, and nationalities. Yet after some discussion, the kids thought we should give it a try. To our surprise, it was the high-light of the weekend. One teacher told me that her superior had said the nicest thing to her that she had ever heard at school. The next year I wasn't along for the retreat—but guess what was a featured event? You're right—"spin the bottle"—appreciation time. We are all starved for appreciation.

Create Opportunities to Appreciate. Our responsibility as parents is once again to create opportunities for our children to appreciate others. First, we must practice appreciating our mates and our kids. Have I thanked my husband for some simple thing he does which I often take for granted? Is there a child who is sad? Perhaps I could put a love note in her lunch box or leave one on her pillow. Have I told my son lately how much I appreciate his sense of humor?

Writing thank-you notes is a good opportunity to train our children in being appreciators. Not many children like to write thank-you notes! Neither do adults. Yet it is an important way to show appreciation. Have the kids keep a list of Christmas and birthday gifts. Set a reason-able date by which all thank-you notes should be written. Begin this when they are just learning to write. For a small child, it may be one sentence and a picture, but he's learning the principle of graciousness. It is so irritating to send a teenager or an adult a gift year after year and never receive one word of response. You feel like they could care less.

Whenever anyone does something thoughtful, it is appropriate to send a note or give a call to thank them. Perhaps someone fixed you a meal or loaned you their home. Thank them. This is one trait that children will not naturally pick up simply because their parents are diligent in their own thank-yous. Kids need to be told why it's important and held accountable to do it.

When you receive similar notes from others, share them at the dinner table with your family. It will reinforce with your kids how much it means to be thanked. Have a family member pray for the writer. Appreciate the memories that the letter evokes.

Honor Your Parents. God's fifth commandment to us is, "Honor your father and your mother" (Exodus 20:12). Part of honoring our parents comes in appreciating them. When did we last write and thank our own parents for some specific things they have done for us? In an age that encourages adults to overcome the damage that their dysfunctional parents did to them, it can become easy to dwell on the negative. No parents are perfect, and often ours did the best they were able, considering the families in which they grew up. Hardly any parent tries to do a bad job in parenting. No matter what our parents did or did not do, they need our appreciation for the little things they did do right. It's part of honoring them. If we want our children to honor us, then they must see us honoring our parents. Tell your children some of the things you appreciate about your own parents and grandparents. Not only does this help them get to know their family better, it also illustrates to them an appreciative spirit.

Appreciation is a wonderful antidote to discouragement. As reasons for discouragement increase, the need for appreciation increases. There is a clear parallel in our own relationship with the Lord. When I am discouraged in spirit, a time of praise to God for who He is—He knows, He understands, He is in charge, He desires good—will lift my spirit. And thanking Him for what He has done in the past—for protecting me, for providing that thing I needed, for showing me what to do in that time of indecision—gives me hope for the future.

When I, in turn, appreciate another for *who she is and for what she does*, she is encouraged, and I grow in developing a servant's heart.

3. Respect

The dictionary defines *respect* as "to feel or show honor or esteem for, to show consideration for."[1]

When I was young there was one sure way to make my father very mad; that was to talk back to my mother. Many times I heard him say, "Do not talk to your mother like that." And I was punished when I did. At the time, it made me mad, but it also made me proud to see my dad stand up for my mom and increased my respect for him as well as for her.

Most children will attempt to speak rudely to their parents, but it must not be tolerated. If it is tolerated in the home, it will become a habit at school and later in the workplace. We must watch our own language. Do I speak kindly to my mate and to my children?

Children will pick up many habits, good and bad, from what they see their parents do. However, we cannot expect our children to catch their lessons from observation alone. Clear explanation and illustration is vital in training them to be respectful.

We role play manners from time to time.

"It's important to look someone in the eye and put your hand out to shake theirs when you meet them," I say, and we practice the look and the shake.

Some of our other favorites are:

- Stand and speak when an adult enters the room.
- Walk your friends to the door when they leave your house.
- Thank the driver for giving you a ride.
- Thank the host for the meal.
- Wait until everyone is finished and you have asked permission to be excused before you leave the table.
- Address adults as Mr. or Mrs. unless they tell you otherwise.
- Always speak to someone when you pass them. Call them by name if you know it.

But what if you or your child is shy? Being shy is all right, being rude is not. It may be more difficult for a quiet person to speak to others, but it is still the polite action to take and can be learned. Shyness must not be allowed to become an excuse for rudeness.

Sixteen-year-old Christine has been a good example to my kids. When she sees me in the hall at school, she says, "Hello, Mrs. Yates." I tell my kids that she makes me feel good. It doesn't hurt to remind children that adults have feelings, too. Christine makes me feel important. Another child I know well will walk right by me without ever speaking; he makes me feel sad.

The junior high years are the most difficult to teach manners. It's an awkward time for the kids, and nothing feels right to them. Be patient, be persistent, and don't give in to discouragement. We are building for the future, and in a few years, those kids who caused us to feel like failures may become polite, kind adults.

And then there are table manners. Table manners seem to have disappeared with our fast-food/microwave generation. And yet family mealtime can be a wonderful celebration, the coming together at the end of the day to share the events of the day.

Table manners are important because I want my children to be at ease in whatever situation God chooses to place them. They may need to know how to dine with kings and presidents or how to be comfortable in an impoverished hut. We do not know what God has in store, but we can prepare them to feel at ease in the most formal as well as the most informal situations.

Occasionally, we eat in our dining room. We use the best china and the nicest linens and pretend that we are dining at the White House. During the meal, we remind one another of proper manners. Making a game out of the training infuses a spirit of fun into what could be a nagging session.

Respect is a habit that is developed daily in little ways. When we, as parents, take time to offer respect to others, our behavior will encourage other family members to practice this small but significant habit.

4. Generosity

Money, time, things, talents, and relationships are five resources we must be willing to share.

A small child with a handful of candy is apt to hold it tightly in his tiny fist, so tightly that occasionally little streams of chocolate creep between the stubby fingers and drip over his clothes and hands. An older child with a lovely butterfly in her outstretched palm tenderly coaxes it to fly away. Stretching her arm out with fingers flat, she delights when the new creature takes to its wings and soars away.

Our natural tendency is to hold on to our possessions with tightly clenched fists. Occasionally, a portion slips out to be shared, but more often it is held closely in our hands. True joy comes, however, when we open our palms and release our resources to God to be used freely for others.

Money. Whenever we hear a sermon or lecture on giving, our thoughts turn first to giving in terms of money. This is probably the most obvious expression of generosity, but it is only one means of generosity. Yet, it is a tangible way to begin to become families with outstretched palms rather than clenched fists.

Before we were married, a wise older couple challenged us to open a new checking account that was a special account—a tithe account into which we would put 10 percent of everything that came into the house. The monies in this account would be used only for giving away to ministries or to people in need. The challenge would be to increase the percentage over the years. This idea has brought us much joy. We avoid the dilemma of deciding how much to give to God's work; it's already decided. We have great fun dispersing the money in the account, and we continue to be challenged to increase the percentage. Friends of ours with a modest income have increased their giving to 20 percent. We are way behind them, but their generosity encourages us.

Our children should be taught from an early age that the tithe (10 percent) is the norm. Our small kids put in a jar 10 percent of their allowance and any other money they earn. Our big kids write checks to the ministries of their choice. Occasionally as a family, we will give an extra gift for a special need. Inevitably we are the ones enriched.

It is great fun to give something anonymously. A single parent who is a close family friend was in desperate financial need. One morning she opened her mail to discover two cashier's checks totaling two thousand dollars. There was no note or any reference to the giver. In seeing God overwhelmingly answer her need through an unknown person, her faith was encouraged. And we saw firsthand the blessing brought by an anonymous gift.

Time. The most valuable commodity in the future will not be money but time, according to some analysts. Already in many instances, it is easier to write a check than to give an hour. Even those who aren't wealthy sometimes feel they have more money than time and not much of either.

With so many choices on how to spend our time and too many needs to be met, it's easy to be depressed before we even look at our "daytimer." We become very protective of our schedules. This is not necessarily bad, but we must take care that we do not clench "our time" too tightly in our fists. Reexamining our priorities in light of our schedules will enable us to discern the best way to spend our time. (See chapter 3.) We must daily give our schedules to God and allow Him to alter them.

Recently I realized I had become selfish with my time. I had set goals to accomplish for the day, and I was inflexible. Subtly, I began to view people as interruptions, and I became unpleasant to be around. I was unconsciously tightening my fists around "my time," and I was unwilling to open myself to unexpected needs.

"Forgive me, Lord," I prayed. "Make me open to your divine interruptions. Give me back a love for people. Help me view delays as Your divine opportunities for me."

"I'm too busy" is probably the most common and the most accurate statement of our generation. We already hear our children mimic us; they are also too busy for this or that.

Developing little disciplines of *giving time* will help us open our fists. Take time with a child to call on an elderly neighbor. Offer to do some handy work for a single parent. Have a lonely child to a tea party. In the small disciplines of life, big lessons of character are learned.

Things. "It's mine, give it back," is a cry heard daily in thousands of homes of toddlers. Learning to share is a hard lesson for all because we want to *keep* not *share*. We consciously teach small children to share; their need is so obvious. But as we grow, we learn to rationalize our selfishness until it's harder to recognize and easier to deny. It is helpful to be aware of this tendency and to ask occasionally, "Am I holding my possessions too tightly, or am I offering them with open hands?"

Giving in small ways prepares one to be generous in bigger ways. Have a child make a picture to give away. Give away a toy that has been outgrown. Make a gift of a dish or picture that a friend has admired. Give the use of a vacation house.

A friend of ours started a car-giving business. He receives cars that people no longer need, fixes them up, and gives them to others in need. Instead of selling or trading in their autos, folks donate them to Roger, and he gives them away. His generosity has blessed countless people.

A couple of mothers in our community have developed a "Prom Dress" lending network. Mothers and daughters make available to one another dressy dresses as the need arises. Each of us saves money, but more importantly, we do not hold on to our possessions too closely. When something is borrowed, we return it in clean condition. Not only is this true of dresses but also of autos, homes, and other items that are loaned. We use the principle, "Leave it better than you found it." That's simple common courtesy.

Talents. Twice a year I host a potluck dinner in my home for approximately ninety people, the newcomers' class at our church. A week before the event my phone inevitably rings. Peggy is on the line to ask me if I would like her to bring a centerpiece for my table. She works part-time in a florist shop and is gifted in flower arranging. I'm not, and the generous gift of her talents encourages me.

God has given to every person unique gifts that are to be used in the building up of the body. (Ephesians 4:16.) Part of growing in generosity involves discovering our gifts and generously using them for others.

Perhaps you have a natural gift of organization. How might this be used in your church or your neighborhood? Are you a good listener? Possibly God is developing your gift of counseling. How might He use this gift to help others? Does your young child show unusual concern for hurting people? Perhaps he has the gift of compassion. Share this insight with his teacher. Encourage him to reach out to the unpopular kids in his classes.

Our role as parents is to study our children. Notice their interests and watch for hints of special talents. Allow room to try out different interests. Encourage them and praise them. Remember that God has given to each special gifts. Their gifts may be very different from what we would have chosen, but they are exactly right for this particular child. Our job is to help them blossom and to train them to be generous in the use of their gifts.

Relationships. "I won't be your friend if you are going to be hers!" This is frequently heard in a fourth grade classroom.

Children are possessive of friendships, but so are adults. A young man dating a girl was overheard telling her whom she was allowed to spend time with and whom she was to avoid.

Giving in small ways prepares one to be generous in bigger ways. Have a child make a picture to give away. Give away a toy that has been outgrown

---

We long for close relationships, and when we finally find one, it can be hard to share. Yet relationships should be built on trust and not held by jealousy.

We have had many talks in our family about sharing friendships. I have asked the teachers of my young children to let me know if they are being possessive of friends in a way that hurts others. We have comforted our teens when they have felt left out of the "in group." To be excluded from some groups is good, but the message here is that we must help our children become those who share friendships with open arms rather than pulling them into exclusive circles.

Our friend Larry talked to us for ages about his best friend Bob. Finally an opportunity arose for my husband to meet Bob. Larry, who knew both Bob and John, could not wait for the two of them to know each other. Now the three men are best friends, all because Larry shared a precious friendship.

Generosity with *money, time, things, talents,* and *relationships* springs from a thankful heart. No matter what we have, if we are thankful then we will be generous.

5. Prayer

First Samuel 12:23 says, "Far be it from me that I should sin against the LORD by ceasing to pray for you."

In each of Paul's letters, he always tells of his prayers for his friends. In prayer for his friends, Paul experiences his greatest joy.

Prayer is something anybody can do. Rich or poor, young or old, ill or healthy, we can all pray. My elderly neighbor, Edith, has been in bed for over a year now. Yet she told me in a halting voice last week that every day she prays for the six families that live on our street. My grandmother died when she was ninety-two. In her last years, she had suffered a stroke, but still she prayed. On my final visit with her, she wanted to pray for each of her twelve grandchildren.

A nurse in the newborn ward of the hospital prays for each infant she holds. She may be the only person ever to pray for that child. Yet God is faithful, and He will hear her prayers for this small infant and answer them. A mother prays whenever she sees a school bus for the kids on the bus.

The greatest sacrifice that we can make for another person is to pray for them.

In his letter to his friends at Philippi, Paul describes the core of a servant's heart:

> Do nothing from selfishness or empty conceit, but with humility of mind let each of you regard one another as more important than himself; do not merely look out for your own personal interests, but also for the interests of others. (Philippians 2:3–4)

PURSUING THE SERVANT'S HEART

As we seek to become people with servant's hearts, there are two final things to keep in mind.

The Clue-In Principle

In our attempts to create opportunities for service, it is helpful to use what I call the "clue-in principle." Perhaps a young son has had a difficult day at school. Clue in his big brother and ask him to invite his little brother to play ball with him. Is a big sister discouraged about a relationship? Clue in a younger sister. Perhaps she can help you make cookies and leave them with a love note on big sister's pillow.

Is Dad under pressure at work? Clue the kids in, asking them to be especially thoughtful when he gets home tonight. Maybe he needs someone to do some of his chores; possibly he needs to be left alone to some peace and quiet Is a teenager in a bad mood? A quick call to Dad at the office will warn him of the need for caution when he gets home.

As we adopt the clue-in principle in families, we will learn to think this way in our other relationships. Is there a single parent under pressure in the neighborhood? Cook a meal for her so she doesn't have to worry about dinner. Did a buddy at school lose an election? Maybe your daughter could write her an encouraging note.

Cluing in one another helps us become sensitive to the needs of others and is a valuable tool in cultivating a servant's hearts.

I Am Not God

That I am not God is obvious. But sometimes, when I see the many needs around me, I get frustrated or I feel guilty. I just can't seem to meet everyone's need. I cannot fx someone's situation. I feel guilty be cause I have no more resources. I am ashamed because I am exhausted and have no more to give. It's time to admit that I am really frustrated because I want to 'be God"—to fix things—and I'm not able. My pride is hurt because I have come to the place where I must say, "God, I can't! And He cheers.

A friend gave us a card that reads, "Do not feel totally, personally, irrevocably responsible for everything. That's My job. Love, God." This is the case for some of us who are overcommitted in responding to the needs around us.

For others, the opposite extreme is true. We are fearful. We don't think we can really help someone, and our fear inhibits the development of a servant's heart. Instead, we desire to be served. So we wait paray lyzed, immobilized because we aren't God. We need to say, "I can't, but I m available, God. And I'll begin in faith to take specific steps to care."

We will not become people who serve overnight; it's a lifelong process. But it begins and grows with small steps taken daily. Little habits developed and cultivated produce the big heart of a servant.

FOCUS QUESTIONS

Meditate on John 13:1–17

1. Why did Peter object to Jesus' washing his feet? How did Jesus respond? What is the message here for you?

2. What three specific steps can you take this week to serve your mate, your child, and someone else?

3. What is one way in which you can begin to help your children cultivate servants' hearts?

Meditate on 1 Peter 4:8–11, making it a personal prayer.

> *The LORD your God is in your midst,*
> *A victorious warrior.*
> *He will exult over you with joy,*
> *He will be quiet in His love,*
> *He will rejoice over you with shouts of joy.*
> *(Zephaniah 3:17)*

COURAGE
(Susan)

SEVEN

*Courage is the first of human qualities
because it is the quality which guarantees all others.*

WINSTON CHURCHILL

*T*ears streamed down my face as I gasped for breath between sobs.
Desperately I tried to pray and to recite familiar Bible verses. John's
damp hand held mine as he, too, prayed and wept.

It was past midnight, and we were in the hospital waiting as our son
Chris underwent a CAT scan to determine the extent of his injuries. He
was irrational, and we could hear him screaming. The neurosurgeon had
told us that his brain was swelling and his skull was most likely frac-
tured. He did not know what the prognosis would be.

Several hours earlier Chris had been swinging on a bar in our basement. Higher and higher he went until he was almost parallel with the
ceiling. And right then the bar broke sending him crashing headfirst
onto the cement floor. By the time the ambulance reached the hospital,
he was incoherently thrashing and crying out in pain.

Now as we waited, I felt paralyzed with fear. Would he be brain
damaged? Would he die? So many terrifying questions and no answers.
I didn't know if I could stand this agony of waiting while my imagination ran rampant with horrible "what if's."

Since it was the middle of the night, we were the only people standing in the long, dark hall outside the X-ray unit. The bleak silence was
oppressive and only fed my sense of desperation.

Gradually, I became aware of a slight movement at the end of the
hall. Through my tears I noticed a hunched over shape moving slowly
toward us. As the figure came closer, I realized that it was the cleaning

woman slowly pushing her cart full of mops and brushes up the hall. Her bent shape reflected the strain of the midnight work shift at the hospital. Struggling with my own emotions, I didn't pay any more attention to the old woman until I felt a hand placed awkwardly on my shoulder.

"Do not worry," she said in broken English. "Your son will be all right. I will pray for him."

Tears of gratitude overwhelmed me, and I mumbled thanks as she continued her shuffle up the corridor.

Throughout Chris's recovery (which was complete), many friends prayed with us and visited him in the hospital. Their love was such an encouragement, and yet I found that the gentle touch and prayer of the cleaning woman had the most profound effect on me. Often my thoughts returned to her. Who was she? What country did she come from? Did she have a family? Why did she do what she did?

She did not know anything about me. She did not know if I would be offended by her outreach. I wasn't her responsibility. She could have avoided me. She could have angered me. She had no way of knowing how I would respond to her, and she may have been afraid. But she overcame fear, she determined to do what was right, and she took a risk. She ministered to me.

She was a woman of *courage*.

When we think of courage, our immediate mental picture might be that of John Wayne or Rambo blazing through the woods. Or it might be a news headline describing the daring rescue of a drowning victim by a passerby. Or it may be a soldier bravely leading his troops into the thick of battle. While these are certainly courageous acts, they are not likely to be a part of our daily routines.

Courage is far more than a split-second decision to save a life. It is bravery, fearlessness, fortitude, valor, boldness, nerve, pluck, determination, endurance, tenacity, and so on. Courage expresses itself in sticking with a mundane job when you want to quit, staying with a difficult marriage when you'd rather walk out, getting on an airplane when you're scared silly, reaching out to someone when he might reject you, or taking the minority stand on a highly unpopular issue.

Courage is everywhere in our daily lives and is the catalyst to all of the other traits we are trying to develop. *Character without courage is empty. Courage is what enables us to act on our convictions.*

Recently, we were at the beach with two other couples that are good friends of ours. John and I asked each of them to share with us the three people who they would say were personal heroes (or positive role mod-

---

Character without courage is empty. Courage is what enables us to act on our convictions.

---

els) to them. These people could be dead or alive. We listed every person that was mentioned. They ranged from Abraham Lincoln to an adult Christian friend. Then we each told what traits we most admired in the persons we had chosen. People were picked that exhibited many different worthwhile traits. One was impressed by brilliance, another by endurance, and so on. Yet there was one trait that was commonly shared by every person that was chosen: courage. Courage gave life to all of the other traits.

Courage is respected and sought by everyone and is available to any individual regardless of social status, accomplishments, or even faith. But there is one common factor that each of us must also deal with: fear.

THE RELATIONSHIP OF COURAGE AND FEAR

Is fear the opposite of courage? Not at all. Is fear necessary for courage? Absolutely. Too often, a person who is afraid is thought to be lacking in courage or in guts. Instead, when we look fear in the face and press on, courage takes hold.

There are "good" fears, and there are "bad" fears. It is good to teach a child to fear a hot stove. It is necessary to instill fear into your toddler of the busy street in front of the house. A healthy fear of the evil influence of the wrong crowd is necessary for your teenager. And Scripture teaches us that we are to fear or to reverence God.

On the other hand, there are many unnecessary but real fears that paralyze us in our daily lives. Courage rises when we try to have these fears work for us rather than against us.

We fear rejection, failure, the unexpected, pain, death, disaster, embarrassment, being found out, not being in control, broken relationships, new experiences. Maybe you fear that you'll turn out like your parents, make the same mistakes with your children that they did with theirs. Or you fear you cannot live up to their expectations. We can all add to the list.

Our fear comes from many sources. Fears grow from past experiences, from fertile imaginations, and from society in general. Fear is a constant challenge which confronts us as long as we live in this world.

How we handle fear will determine whether it is used to build our courage or to paralyze us. Usually we will either *deny* fear, *be overcome by* fear, or *face* fear.

There is something about us that wants to *deny* our fears.

My friend Anna has had a hard time. Her husband left her and her two young children. It was a complete shock to her and to those of us who knew the family. For several months, Anna was in a real state of depression. Her future was uncertain. There was no money. She had no job. She had to make some difficult decisions. In the midst of her misery, she began to drink more regularly to ease the pain. Almost imperceptibly the amount of liquor grew. Initially, Anna chose to deny that she was afraid and that she had a problem. "This is a hard time for me, and a drink will help me calm down," she rationalized.

And yet as time went by, Anna began to drink more and more. One evening as she reached for a beer, her young son looked up and said, "How many does that make, Mom?"

Startled by his question, Anna realized that she did *not* know. Was she drinking too much? What should she do?

Her son's question was the first of a series of events that caused Anna to take a hard look at the amount she was drinking. She realized that she could no longer deny her fear about the future nor cover it up with alcohol. She began to attend Alcoholics Anonymous, and she gave up liquor completely. Instead of denying her fears, she faced them. It was a courageous choice.

A second response to fear is simply to *be overcome by* it. Recently this happened to me. Several summers ago while we were on a family vacation at the beach, I became seriously ill. A rush to the hospital in the middle of the night led to emergency surgery which revealed that I had been bleeding internally for several days from a ruptured ovarian cyst. While the surgery was successful, I was quite sick because my stomach did not react positively to all the interference. However, I recovered, came home, and put the horrible experience behind me. At least, I thought I did. But the following summer when we got to the beach, I began to panic. I was sure my stomach hurt, and I wondered when I should go to the hospital. And I became afraid that one of the children would become seriously ill. I was overcome by fear.

Nothing happened that summer or the next, except that the fears kept returning every time we went on vacation. At first, I didn't tell John. I was too embarrassed. And I wasn't honest with God about how I was feeling either. I was ashamed that I couldn't control my emotions. And the fears made me angry. Even today I still struggle with a sense of panic on vacations, but I am learning to *face* my fears, rather than be overwhelmed by them, and to give them to a loving God who understands.

Fear is a natural human emotion, but God does not want it to control us. I believe that God wants us to accept the reality of this emotion in our lives, and He wants to use it to help us grow. "When I am afraid, I will put my trust in Thee," says David in Psalm 56:3.

"Let not your heart be troubled, nor let it be fearful," Jesus gently tells us in John 14:27.

Scripture could be viewed as a biography of fearful people. Fear is not new; it has been a problem since the Garden of Eden. God knows our fears, and He understands.

A favorite passage of mine is Psalm 139. In it David talks of God's intimate knowledge of each of us. God knows what we are thinking even before we speak a single word. That can be both embarrassing and comforting. It's embarrassing to think that I can't hide even my most awful thoughts from God, yet comforting when I remember that even though He knows every thought, He still loves me totally and completely. This realization should enable us to be completely honest with God about our fears. He knows them anyway, and that gives us the freedom to speak of them to Him.

Thus, the first step in overcoming our fears is to acknowledge them. Then we must give them to God. He wants to take all of our fears on His shoulders, and He will give us His peace (Philippians 4:6–7). There is no fear too big or too trivial for God. He will take away our fears, but we must give them to Him first, and continue to give them to Him as they reappear.

Small children are refreshingly honest about their fears. Bedtime is a wonderful time for honest conversation. Perhaps it postpones going to bed, but I've found that some of my most precious conversations happen when I'm curled up with a child on her bed. Snuggling close to a parent, a child might share something that she fears. Perhaps it's the first day at a new school or an upcoming sleep-over away from home. This is a wonderful opportunity for Mom or Dad to reassure the child that her fear is normal and that Jesus understands it. Recall a time when you had a similar fear, and share it with the child. Then pray together, giving the fear to God and asking for His peace.

In my own life, I've found it helpful on occasion to have small "ceremonies" in which I picture myself giving Jesus a package which is my fear. Often I take it back and worry some more, until once again frustrated, I give the fear back to God. And I picture Him with eyes full of love gently saying, "Susan, my child, I want to take your fears. I love you. Rest in My love and let Me have your worries."

Often it helps to share your fears with a friend and have them pray for you. Once I shared a fear with a close friend. Her response was, "I will pray for you concerning this fear every day for the next month. Don't you even think about it or pray about it. Let me carry this for you."

Her willingness to carry my burden and her persistent prayers gave me a deep sense of relief.

If you are overcome by deep-seated anxieties, seek out a wise Christian counselor for help. In addition, a medical doctor may discover a physiological reason that is contributing to your fear which can be helped with medication. Our purpose is not to address fear in depth. There are others far better qualified to deal with this extensively.

Our purpose is to encourage you to ask God to use your fear to increase your courage. When we recognize our fear and consciously give it to God, He will give us the courage to enable us to burst through the barriers that cause us to fear.

BURSTING THROUGH BARRIERS

When I think of bursting through barriers, a picture comes to mind of the great steeplechase horse races. Organized steeplechasing dates back to the 1830s in Europe. Today the most famous chase is the Grand

National in England. This race consists of four and one-half miles with thirty different jumps. Some of the jumps are over five feet high. So hazardous is the race that few horses actually finish the course. The rider and horse must conquer brush fences, stone walls, and even fences followed immediately by eight-foot-wide ditches. It is, indeed, a danger-

---

*P*ersonal security, clear convictions, and a
sense of destiny are foundational elements
that will stimulate the development
of courage in our families.

---

ous sport. There are many barriers for the horse and rider to burst through, but a few things are absolutely fundamental before they can conquer the obstacles.

The rider must understand horses. He has to have good balance and coordination. He needs to be able to judge distances, and he has to have a keen sense of timing. Without these and other foundational skills, he would be unable to conquer the many barriers in the race.

In a similar way, there are three foundational elements that we must develop if we are to burst through fear barriers and become people of courage. *Personal security, clear convictions,* and *a sense of destiny* are foundational elements that will stimulate the development of courage in our families.

1. Personal Security

"I am a promise. I am a possibility. I am a promise with a capital P." So goes a wonderful song by Bill Gaither. Sung in part by a small child, the message is abundantly clear: "I am special." If you ask my five-year-old nephew Catlin who he is, he may reply, "I am a blessing and a treasure from Jesus." His mother has taught him this, and in the future when he goes through times of loneliness and rejection, this phrase will spring from his young memory to give him comfort.

Knowing that God loves me no matter what I do is fundamental to a sense of security. Only His love never fails. Those from unhappy homes must fall back over and over again on the faithfulness of God. But even those from happy homes will know that their parents are not perfect. Ultimately, our security rests in being God's child, for He alone is the perfect parent.

Personal security means knowing who you are, feeling that you are accepted, and having the assurance that someone believes in you. This type of security gives us the ability to attempt difficult things, to overcome bad habits, to hang in there when everything goes wrong. That's courage.

As a little boy, my husband remembers his mother telling him often how special he was. She also told him stories of family members from long ago. In her positive way, she would point out unique, admirable qualities in different family members. Unconsciously he came to believe that he was part of a very special family. This added to his security.

Our friends Beth and Jeff have adopted two Korean children. Over and over again, Beth tells the children how glad she is that God chose her and Jeff to be their parents. Being adopted is extra special because you are especially chosen by your parents. They want you very much, and you become a part of a special family. Family security is related to the concept of covenant. A covenant is an agreement and a bond between persons that is permanent. Unlike contracts, covenants cannot be broken; they last forever.

Security grows when we are committed to living under the covenant. Our marriages are permanent; we will work through whatever problems may arise. Our commitment to our children is forever—no matter what they do. It is a good thing to stress this again and again to our kids because the world is preaching such a different message.

This sense of family security will give us the courage to admit when we are wrong.

Recently, I said something to John that was really ugly. Also I had twisted the truth about a small issue to make me look good. Now it was a small thing, so I reasoned I could ignore it. Or I could admit my sin and ask my husband's forgiveness. Which would take more courage?

It takes courage to go to another and admit wrongs and ask forgiveness. Our pride is in a tug-of-war against our courage. But recognizing this battle and taking the right step will enable courage to have a greater pull in our lives.

Our homes should be places where a banner hangs over the house which says, "Here you are loved forever—no matter what."

Last week Allison, who's eighteen, had a bad day at work. She found out that she had incorrectly entered several pages of data on the computer in her office. Another very busy person was going to have to take several hours to undo her mistake. In addition, everything else seemed to go wrong at her job. It was just one of those days we all have when we wish we could crawl in a hole.

The twins and I prayed for Allison, and the girls put notes and M&M's on her pillow saying that they loved her and they thought she was a good big sister. Acceptance? Assurance? You bet. With that backing, she will be encouraged to burst through the barrier of feeling like a failure on the job and will learn how to use the data base correctly.

A sense of personal security will give us the confidence to face and conquer difficult things.

Sharing our battles with someone else encourages the growth of our courage.

Last winter the twins and I went snow skiing. I had not been in twenty years, and they had never skied. The slopes we were on had only one course open—the intermediate level with a vertical drop of 1,053 feet.

We were scared, but we decided to try it. We talked about how frightened we each were, and yet we were determined to conquer this slope. There was a sense of camaraderie among us because of our common fear. The girls especially liked the fact that I was really scared. It was a very long day—filled with laughter and with tears. Our bottoms became wet and sore, but by the end of the day we were skiing! Sharing together in fear and in victory increased our confidence and stimulated the development of courage.

Knowing we are loved, feeling we are accepted, and being assured that someone believes in us will give us a sense of security that encourages the growth of courage.

2. Clear Convictions

A sense of feeling secure is important, but alone it will not enable the growth of courage. We must have a clear sense of what we believe and why. A person without clear convictions will learn simply to give in to the greatest source of pressure rather than courageously do what is right.

A new "god" seems to have appeared in our society—the "god" of tolerance. Tolerance is now viewed as a positive, noble trait in nearly every situation. A dangerous subtle message has arisen that says, "If you are intolerant, then you aren't loving and thus how could you really be a Christian?" Desperately we do whatever we can in order not to offend someone. We are so afraid of being labeled intolerant in our convictions that we become wishy-washy, having no firm values at all. A valueless society is being built for the sake of tolerance.

Although God loves us completely, He does not tolerate any and every kind of behavior. In His love for us, He has established very clear values for us. They are laid down in Scripture and have been illustrated in the lives of saints for thousands of years. He has given us clear instructions on how we should live.

God's Word is full of nonnegotiables for family living: the Ten Commandments, commitment to Christ as our first priority, the sanctity of marriage, and others mentioned in previous chapters. These nonnegotiables form the basis of our convictions.

There are also many "negotiables" in a believer's life. Do we home school our kids, or do we send them to Christian schools or to public schools? There is not one right answer. The answer depends on the needs of the child and the available resources.

For many things in life there is not one best way. But there are also many things about which God is very clear. These clear values must form the basis of our families' convictions.

Having clear convictions will help us overcome indecisiveness. A couple of months ago there was an article in the *Washington Post* headlined, "Two Who Dared to Take the Stand." The story described two Human Services employees who chose to expose the dangerous deficiencies of the city's Child and Family Service Division for which they worked.

One of the workers, Ms. Scott, said,

> There was a lot of hesitancy on my part about testifying. I thought, *Why should I put my career on the line?* But then I thought: *It's not fair to the children and it's not fair to me.* The line workers were very supportive. I kept hearing the word *courage* being thrown around, and I kept thinking: *But this is no big deal. This is just the truth.*[1]

It was "just the truth," but Ms. Scott's courage came into play when she chose to act on the truth. Treading a safe path would have been easier—doing a good job herself and trying to ignore the injustices done by others. But her convictions of right and wrong forced her to make a decision. She had to choose to do something or to do nothing. She decided to do something. That's courage.

Having clear convictions encourages endurance.

Mark came home in tears the other day from his tennis lesson. "Mom," he cried, "the other boys just laughed at me. They said I'm not

---

A person without clear convictions will learn simply to give in to the greatest source of pressure rather than courageously do what is right.

---

any good. Just because I'm the youngest they make fun of me. I'm never going back to those lessons again."

Mark's mother comforted him and then left him alone to sort things out for himself. Later that night as she was tucking him in bed, he said, "Mom, I've decided that I'm going back to tennis. I can't let those boys take away my opportunity to have fun and learn how to play tennis."

Mark's convictions that he did not want to be a quitter gave him the courage to endure. As he sticks to his tennis, he will learn valuable lessons of endurance which will prepare him for adulthood.

Clear convictions enable us to be able to take a stand.

Two thirteen-year-olds went to the movies. Their parents had approved the movie, albeit with some hesitancy. As the girls quietly watched the opening scene, the violence became more and more graphic. Tami began to feel uncomfortable. She didn't really want to watch the rest of the movie, but she did not know how her friend felt. Finally she decided that she had to leave, so she told her friend, who was actually feeling the same way but was too afraid to admit it. They went out and phoned their parents to come pick them up.

It took courage for my young friend Tami to take a stand. And her wise parents praised her for it. Will this encourage her to stand strong in the future? Definitely. She won't always be praised for the stands she takes, but she is learning that courage means standing for one's convictions.

A high school science teacher was lecturing on the amazing breakthroughs in genetic engineering. As she discussed the potential of this vast research, she remarked that one benefit would be the ability to detect genetic malformations in the smallest embryos and eliminate the embryo, thereby preventing much pain for people. As she continued, a quiet girl struggled in turmoil with what was being said. Finally, she could not remain silent any longer, and she raised her hand.

"I'm sorry, Mrs. —-, but I disagree with you. You see, my sister Sarah, who is seven, is profoundly retarded. But I am glad she was born. She has taught my family what it means to really care for each other." Taking a stand for truth is a step of courage.

Clear convictions make it easier to recognize and resist temptation.

A friend visiting from England shared with us recently a troublesome encounter he had with a close Christian brother. The "brother" had a new angle on a business project. So excited was he about the endless possibilities that this new angle would open up that he didn't notice the puzzled expressions on our friend's face. Finally our friend said to the other man, "But don't you realize that this new angle borders on being unethical?"

The success potential had overwhelmed the conviction of integrity, and temptation had slipped in disguised as a creative business decision—a new angle. Having firm convictions and keeping them in front of us will help us be alert when temptation comes our way.

A decorated military officer recently spoke at our public high school to the students who had made the honor role. His talk was on leadership. He said that the higher you get in rank, the more successful you become, then the greater and more subtle the temptations. He listed absolute integrity as the number one criterion for leadership. Yet he was quick to say that an ability to withstand adversity was crucial, because the more successful you are the more adversity you will face. The temptation to compromise is ever-present for successful people. Every time you say no to the temptation, another step of courage is taken.

3. A Sense of Destiny

We might have a sense of security. We may have strong convictions, but we can still lack courage. Security and convictions alone can cause us to become self-focused and frustrated or isolated without hope. What is needed is a sense of destiny.

We need to know that God has created each of us for a very special purpose. Our task cannot be done by anyone else in the whole world.

Many people walk about depressed because they have no hope. Young children give up on their schoolwork or with trying to make a friend or even on pleasing their parents. Failure has become such a companion that hope has been lost. What our world needs is a new generation of people with hope—hope that springs from personal security, that is rooted in conviction, and that is driven by a sense of destiny.

A sense of destiny is the third foundational element necessary for the growth of courage, and it takes root when we have someone who believes in us. We can encourage a sense of destiny in our loved ones simply by communicating that we believe in them.

Encouragement is a trait that is sorely lacking in our homes, offices, schools, and even churches. Yet God has called us to be encouragers of one another (Hebrews 3:13). To criticize someone or take them for granted is much easier than to encourage them.

Have I taken my child with that easy disposition for granted lately as I have concentrated on his challenging brother? Perhaps I need to tell him what a good ball player he is. Have I told my friend that I think she has a gift of wisdom, that I appreciate her unusual insights? What about the lonely child in the neighborhood? Maybe he needs an adult who will recognize his potential and tell him he has an exciting future ahead. Offers of practical help to encourage his dreams will give him a sense of destiny.

Telling our children that God has a special plan for them encourages a sense of destiny within their spirit. In Ephesians 2:10 (NIV), Paul says, "We are God's workmanship, created in Christ Jesus to do good works, which God prepared in advance for us to do." Simply share this verse with a child and explain to him that he is so unique that God has a special work that's created just for him to do. Watch his anticipation grow, and pray for God to nurture this seed of destiny.

Learning to be a risk taker is an important aspect in developing a sense of destiny. We must be willing to take a risk to try something new. To stick to the familiar instead of risking a new venture is often easier. But risk taking can begin in small areas. Take the training wheels off a child's bike, and watch him risk riding a two-wheeler. Encourage your young teen to run for school office, and watch her give a speech publicly for the first time.

Some children come into the world more willing to take risks while others are by nature more cautious. Our job as parents is to be sensitive to their disposition and encourage them to take wise risks (not foolish chances).

A fear of failure will often prevent us from taking a risk. We must not let failure alone hold us back from this important step of courage. The great Thomas Edison once attempted ten thousand experiments with a storage battery which failed to produce results. When a friend tried to console him he replied, "Why, I have not failed! I've just found ten thousand ways that won't work."[2]

Determining to be a difference maker will also encourage a sense of destiny.

Rod is a very successful orthopedic surgeon. He built his own practice which now includes several associates. A few years ago, however, he realized that he was a little bored with his life. So subtle was his discontent that he didn't recognize it until he attended a conference where the theme was "Becoming difference makers." As Rod heard the speakers and talked to individuals, he was greatly challenged to consider new ways in which he might make a difference for good. He began to pray for God to give him a fresh vision for his life.

Sometime after he returned home, a close friend died of leukemia. In an effort to bring good out of her death, Rod began to help locate bone marrow donors for others in need. He began a whole new organization, Bone Marrow Wanted (BMW), recruited many adults, and began programs in high schools—all in addition to his practice.

Invigorated, enthusiastic, and challenged, Rod has become a new man. He took a risk to step out and be a difference maker—a courageous step that has given him a fresh sense of destiny.

Occasionally, it takes courage to allow God to use our handicaps in being difference makers. Scottie, a young mother of three in our church, has cancer. She has had surgery and is undergoing a heavy treatment of chemotherapy. We are all hopeful for a full recovery. Yet during this difficult time, Scottie has touched our hearts with her courage. She has been the one to take the initiative to reach out to others in similar situations. She calls to encourage them; she comforts the rest of us.

❧   ❧   ❧

As the horse and rider fly over the first fence in the great steeplechase race, the jockey looks ahead to the next barrier. As it becomes clear in the jockey's sight, he has confidence that his horse can take it. His horse is well prepared both from training and from experience in other races. There is always the fear that he will fail, but the possibility of victory gives him the courage to go for it.

A *sense of security, clear convictions,* and *a sense of destiny* enable us to burst through whatever challenges are in front of us. Fear paralyzes; courage energizes. Courage is expressed every time we overcome fear and burst through the barrier facing us. Each step of courage further strengthens us for the challenges ahead.

❧   ❧   ❧

An old cleaning woman in a dark hospital corridor overcame fear, she determined to do what was right, and she took a risk. Her courage was used for good in my life. May our courage grow and become a contagious trait in the lives of those around us and a stimulus to the next generation.

FOCUS QUESTIONS

Meditate on 1 Samuel 25:1–35

1. As you imagine yourself in Abigail's shoes, what are your fears?

   • How did Abigail handle the challenges in front of her?
   • How did God use her courage for good in David's life?

2. What is something in your life that causes you to fear? What do you need to do to "burst through" this barrier of fear?

3. Is there a situation in which a child is coping with fear? Perhaps this is a good time to explain the relationship of fear and courage by sharing with your child a time when you were especially afraid. Talk about the goodness and the power of God.

Meditate on Psalm 33:13–22, thanking God for what He does for you.

> *Be strong and courageous, do not be afraid or tremble at them, for the LORD your God is the one who goes with you. He will not fail you or forsake you.*
> *(Deuteronomy 31:6)*

FAITH
(Susan)

*Faith is the ceasing from all nature's efforts and all other
dependence; faith is confessed helplessness casting itself upon
God's promise and claiming its fulfillment; faith is the putting
of ourselves quietly into God's hands for Him to do His work.*

ANDREW MURRAY

*I*t was Sunday morning. There was not a dry eye among the people
sitting quietly in the historic Falls Church. All eyes were riveted toward
the front where thirteen high school students stood around a large
bearded man whose head was bowed.

"Boris," my husband said, "I baptize you in the name of the Father,
the Son, and the Holy Spirit.

"We receive you into the household of God, confess the faith of
Christ crucified, proclaim His resurrection, and share with us in His
eternal priesthood." [1]

As an unusual applause erupted, John threw his arms around Boris
and gave him a giant bear hug.

Boris and the high school students standing with him were all from
Russia and had been in the U.S. for just two weeks.

Three days earlier we had been on a family vacation when the unexpected phone call came from Jerry, our close friend and church member
who directs Young Life in our area.

"John," he said, "you know that we have had a group of Russian
students staying with families in our church and attending a Young Life
camp. For two weeks their leader, Boris, has been asking many questions about the Christian faith and just last night he decided to give his
life to Christ. His one desire is that he be baptized before he returns

121

home. Could you come home and do it in the service at church on Sunday?"

Boris was a member of the communist party and the vice president of one of the leading colleges in Leningrad. Left behind in Russia were his two daughters and lovely wife. At this particular time in Soviet history, Boris's decision was a courageous one. He did not know how his profession of faith would be received. He wondered if he would lose his job when he returned. Would his friends shun him? Most important, what would his wife and children think of his decision?

At the end of the service, he told John that his biggest desire was that his wife and children come to know Jesus and that he might bring them back to this church to be baptized as well.

Turning his back on the atheistic teachings of his heritage and committing his life to Christ was a dramatic step for Boris. He had no idea how drastically his life would change. He knew little of the teachings of Christ or even how to get to know this God in whom he had just placed his trust. He simply knew that he wanted to know God, and he was willing to place his life in God's hands. He made a life-changing choice.

Long ago, in another land, a battle-weary leader made a similar choice. Joshua had grown weary of the fickleness of the Israelites. Even after experiencing years of God's faithfulness, these Israelites still seemed unable to decide whether to trust in Him or not. Finally, in the most dramatic speech of his career, Joshua challenged his people,

> Choose for yourselves today whom you will serve: whether the gods which your fathers served which were beyond the River, or the gods of the Amorites in whose land you are living; *but as for me and my house, we will serve the LORD.* (Joshua 24:15, emphasis added)

MAKE THE CHOICE

Our son Chris has a T-shirt that says, "Just Do It!" This new slogan has become the "in" phrase of today's youth, and in the process made millions for its creator, the Nike Company.

The first step in cultivating the trait of faith is simply to "just do it"—to make the decision that growing together in relationship to Christ will be a priority for your family. This can be our decision as parents no matter where we are personally in our own journey of faith.

God takes us right where we are. He is far more concerned with our desire to grow in Him than He is with our knowledge or lack of it. Even if our spouse is unwilling to join in this endeavor, God will honor the parent who takes the step alone.

Newlyweds, older adults, young children—anyone can make this decision. The role of a parent is first to make a decision to follow Christ as an individual. Then, with our mates, determine that first and fore-

---

The first step in cultivating the trait of faith is simply to "just do it"—to make the decision that growing together in relationship to Christ will be a priority for your family.

---

most we will follow Christ in our families. But what if my mate is not a believer? God has promised to be our partner, and our families will be sanctified through our faith (1 Corinthians 7:14). Even if our mate does not know Christ, we have the authority and privilege to raise our children to love Him.

Before the marriage, a common decision should be made to commit the marriage and future children to Christ. Two people with a common faith in Christ and a desire to live for Him will have a head start in cultivating families of faith. But it is never too late to begin.

The first step in building families with faith is simply to decide that I want to give my life to Christ and that I will teach my children, as best I know how, to love Him as well.

Second, we must determine to be honest. Our children are not looking for parents with all the answers. They do not require perfect parents. Instead, they need honest parents.

Fred and Barbara had two young girls (ages five and nine) when they became restless in their marriage and with family life in general. Coming from a Christian background, Fred had a sneaking suspicion that their problem was spiritual in nature. As a couple, they had no faith nor had they ever felt the need for one. Now, however, a gnawing dissatisfaction held the potential for either a breakup of the family or a discovery of a genuine faith.

Fortunately for Fred and Barbara, their restlessness ended with both of them coming to faith in Jesus. They made a very clear and serious decision. They explained their decision to the girls, and they, too, expressed a desire to give their hearts to Christ. Fred and Barbara realized that this was a new beginning for the family and that each of them had a lot to learn. As they attended fellowship groups, read the Bible, and began to pray, they discussed with their girls the things they were learning. They were honest in sharing what they did not yet understand. Gradually, changes began to occur in the family. Fred and Barbara sought forgiveness of one another when they said hurtful things. There was no pretense in their spiritual growth. Instead, it was a natural sharing of something important to them. Responding to the positive changes in their parents, the girls began to grow in their faith as well.

Fred and Barbara did not know much about their newfound faith. They made a lot of mistakes. But their children knew their faith was genuine.

Raising kids with faith does not mean that the parents get their act together and then present it to their children. Rather, raising children with faith means that the parents have a hunger to grow and act upon it.

As a parent, you should realize that as Christians we are brothers and sisters with our children. God is our Father, and we are all His children. We are on the same plane as our kids. This is wonderfully freeing and gives us a sense of a corporate journey. Our mutual dependence is to be on God rather than on each other.

Those of us who have accepted Christ personally before we have children often wonder how much pressure we should put on our children to accept Christ. How old should they be? Wouldn't we be manipulating them? What if they were to rebel? Shouldn't we let them grow up and decide for themselves? How can we know what is right to do?

We have found a natural honesty the best approach. When our children were very young, we explained to them that Jesus loved them and had taken away their sins on the cross. He wanted to come into their heart and live there forever. Because it was a special invitation, only they could invite Jesus into their hearts. We explained that this was something they would want to do when they felt they were ready. Then they could come to us and we would pray with them if they liked, or they could pray by themselves. Each of our five children had asked Christ into their lives by the time they were four. They still have memories, albeit vague, of the time. I wrote it down for them in their baby books as a remembrance.

Now let me quickly say that my children have not lived perfect lives, certainly there have been highs and lows in the growth of their faith. The same is true of their parents' faith! Children who make decisions for Christ at an early age will have many times of recommitment throughout their lives. However, the blessing of knowing that Christ is in their life and that He will never leave them gives them the security of belonging. His Holy Spirit has begun work early in their tender hearts, molding them into the people He has created them to be.

DEPENDENCE ON THE FATHER

In raising children with faith, our goal as parents should be the steady turning of our children from dependence upon us to dependence upon their heavenly Father.

We are with them for approximately eighteen years; He is with them for eternity. How then can we bring about this shifting of dependence? Five components will enable us to become more dependent upon God ourselves and to lead our children into this dependence.

1. The Power and Practicality of God's Word

As a young child, I remember trying to read the Bible on different occasions, usually when I had been naughty, had a problem, or for some reason was feeling unusually religious. Inevitably I would begin in Genesis and get to the lists of who begot whom and fall asleep!

In all honesty, I could not see what relevance this book had for me. Not until I was in college and met Ricky did things begin to change.

A strikingly handsome college basketball player, Ricky seemed to have everything going for him. He was interesting and fun. As I got to know him, I became aware of a depth to his personality that I could not explain. He had a deep assurance about his faith and an amazing ability to be able to relate it to ordinary, everyday situations. He was excited about God's Word. I shared my frustrations with him, and he began to teach me how he studied the Bible. We began not in Genesis but in the gospel of Luke. By asking simple questions of the passages, I began to learn how God's Word was relevant to my life.

The secret is asking questions about the Scriptures: What does it say? What does it mean? How does it apply to my life? A reliable study Bible with notes is helpful to understand the historical background and context. Cross-references often help to gain a broader understanding. The acrostic S.P.A.C.E. will help you gain deeper personal insights.

- Sins—Are there any sins described here with which I need to deal?
- Promises—Are there promises here from God to me?
- Attitudes—Does this passage describe attitudes I need to develop?
- Commands—Are there commands here to be obeyed?
- Example—Is there an example here to follow?

At first I felt awkward with this method of Bible study. But as I persisted over a period of time, I grew in confidence and began to realize that God was speaking clearly to me through His Word. Slowly the Scriptures became relevant to my everyday life. Now over twenty years later, I still find that this method of study continues to make God's Word alive for me.

There are literally thousands of promises in the Word of God, but we can't benefit from them unless we learn to take God up on them.

We have a delicious red raspberry patch at our farm that produces fruit twice a year. At this moment, it is fairly bursting with juicy red raspberries. For the last several days, I have been trying to find time to go and pick them, but I haven't gotten to it. They are mine to eat, but I must pick them and pop them into my mouth to enjoy their delicious taste. So it is with God's Word—full of promises for you and for me and for our children, but we have to take God up on His promises in order to benefit from them.

Our family experienced this recently when John's car died, and we did not have the resources to get another. This left us with only one vehicle—a challenging situation with almost five teenagers! At the supper table, John shared the need with the children.

"Kids," he said, "you know how badly we need a car. I don't know how we are going to get one. Philippians 4:19 says, 'And my God will meet all your needs according to his glorious riches in Christ Jesus' (NIV).

"We must take God up on this promise. Let's ask Him to supply our needs."

We prayed together about our need for a car, asking God to show us the way to get another or to show us that we did not need it after all. A week later a local businessman asked John if he had any use for an old company car. Our red Volvo with over two hundred thousand miles on it is a constant reminder to us that God supplies our needs.

Last year was Allison's senior year in high school, a year of big decisions. College loomed ahead, and she did not know where she should go. As a family we began to claim the verse in James 1:5, "If any of you lacks wisdom, he should ask God, who gives generously to all without finding fault, and it will be given to him" (NIV).

We prayed for many months for God to make His perfect will clear to Allison. We regularly made this verse a part of our prayer time. In April, God did give Allison a real peace about the college she should attend. Now, after having been at the University of Virginia for several months, she is clearly in the right place for her.

To appreciate the relevancy of Scripture, consider two types of experiences: *spontaneous* and *planned.*

Spontaneous use of Scripture happens when we claim God's promises as our needs arise. Our red Volvo and Allison's college decision are examples.

Planned studies are set-aside times to dig deeper into God's Word. Ricky taught me how to do this. We should practice both in our own lives and with our children.

Share promises with your kids that are special to you and tell them why. Memorize new ones together and ask God to help you use them in your life. Give each child a Bible to mark. Some good ones are: *International Children's Bible,* New Century Version (Word) for small children, *J. B. Phillips* or *Good News Bibles* for the preteens, and *The Student Bible,* New International Version (Zondervan) for teenagers. New pencils and notebooks are always appreciated for study. For the young children, music provides a delightful way to learn Scripture. Tapes of "G.T. and The Halo Express" (Word) are verses put to music that young kids love.

Set aside a specific time every week for a brief family Bible study. With small children, it should be short. Learn one promise and underline it in your Bible. As the children grow older, take a passage, and after silent reading, let each person share what he or she discovered in the verses.

Family vacations can provide a more relaxed time to study together. This summer while we were at the beach for a week we studied great sea passages. Since the children are ages eleven to eighteen, we were all able to do individual study. John chose one story and one psalm that had something to do with water. We each separated for individual quiet times, then we returned for a time of group sharing.

After reading about a sea storm in Psalm 107:23–32, Libby, reflecting on verse 28, wrote, "There are some times that the Lord frees me from my distress, and I just take it for granted." Oh, the honesty of youth!

One evening after studying the story of Jonah, we experienced a huge storm. Watching the lightning blaze and hearing the roar of an angry surf in the black night made Jonah's predicament come alive in a most dramatic way.

"Wow!" gasped one of the twins. "Now I know why Jonah was scared!"

Creatively taking advantage of spontaneous and planned opportunities to introduce God's Word to our small children instills in them a hunger to initiate their own personal study as they reach the teen years. When they get older, take frequent trips to a local Christian bookstore and let each child pick out a devotional book to guide him in his quiet times. There are many good ones on the market.

Our children's hunger for God's Word will grow when they observe the hunger we have. When they see us spending time in His Word, they will, too. If I want to become a person of faith and I desire for my children to as well, I must make a priority of spending time alone each day in God's Word and in prayer. Raising children with a love for the Bible occurs as the parents take time themselves to learn from God's Word.

2. The Benefits of Prayer

Each August, John and I go away together for a day to do some planning for the coming school year. We take some time to discuss each of our five children in several areas of growth: what are the physical, spiritual, mental, emotional, and social needs of this particular child for the coming year?

A physical need might be better eating habits and less junk food. A mental need would be more discipline in study habits, and so on. We write the needs down, and this list becomes the focus of our prayer time for each child for the coming year.

Several years ago we felt that our son Chris had an important emotional need: he needed to feel he was special. Smack in the middle of five children, he was more likely to feel squashed or insignificant instead of special. And so we began to pray for this eleven-year-old.

In just a few months, Chris had his accident and spent two weeks in the hospital recovering. During this time we shared with him the verse

---

If I want to become a person of faith and I desire for my children to as well, I must make a priority of spending time alone each day in God's Word and in prayer.

---

from Romans 8:28, "And we know that God causes all things to work together for good to those who love God, to those who are called according to His purpose."

Together we prayed for God to bring good from this situation. While he was in the hospital, many friends, teachers, and adults came to visit. Get-well cards soon covered the entire wall by his bed. Finally the day came to bring him home. As we were getting ready to leave, I asked Chris how he thought God had answered our prayer and brought good out of his accident.

He was quiet for a moment and then he said, "Mom, I never knew I was so special before."

Yes, God answers the prayers of parents.

Two common fears. We all want to grow in prayer, yet often we are stopped by two common fears.

We fear that we are unworthy. How can we pray when there is so much in our lives that we know is not right? We must remember that God is our heavenly Father and He desires to communicate with us. He already knows everything in our lives, but still He desires to talk with us. We go to God not because of who we are, but because of who He is.

A second fear is, "What if He doesn't answer? Then my faith or my child's faith will be damaged."

I've found that God answers in three basic ways: yes, no, and wait. Perhaps there is a long silence with the wait. That is hard to take, yet we must remember that God is not hampered by our timetables, and He is not limited to working in ways we can predict. He always does what's best, not necessarily what's fast.

When He answers no, He answers out of love, because He knows what's best for us just as you'd answer no if your three-year-old wanted to play in the street. Or perhaps you'd answer wait when your fourteen-year-old wanted to date. Often we don't understand the answers, but we need to remember that God can be trusted and He always answers out of His love for us. When we explain to our children the different ways that God answers prayers, we reassure them that we can talk to God about anything.

Spontaneous and planned prayer. Beside our breakfast table is a large bulletin board cluttered with photos of friends who live out of town. Each morning at breakfast, the "prayer leader of the day" gets to pray for someone from the board. Also over breakfast, different ones share what they have coming up that day needing prayer. Chris has another geometry test; Susy has student council. Dad has a church budget meeting. (He hates budget meetings!) After a brief time of prayer, there's a mad rush to catch the school bus.

Occasionally, we use a prayer notebook to record special things for which we are praying and how and when God answers. To look back over the past and see the many ways in which God has answered is very encouraging. Flipping through the book recently, I noticed a request for God to send our young nephew Thomas a good friend. Scrawled beside the request were the words, "Yes—Patrick!" The book of Psalms is a beautiful record of the prayers of the children of Israel and God's answers to them. I imagine that when the Israelites were feeling discouraged, they would write a psalm listing specific things God had done in the past. This encouraged them to believe again that He would indeed be faithful in the future and answer their prayers. Psalm 136 is a wonderful example of this.

Keeping a notebook reminds us of God's faithfulness and encourages us to believe He will also answer our current prayers.

Planned prayer times for each family will differ according to family schedules. The important thing is to take a look at your schedule and determine when you can have some brief time together.

Spontaneous prayer occurs simply as the need arises. Often we are made aware of a situation and think, *I'll pray about that later.* Then we forget.

Sometime ago, Allison came into the kitchen, where I was working. She didn't seem to have anything to say, but she just hung around. I have learned that often when teenagers hang around, they have something on their minds, so I asked her what she was thinking. A boy that she had not seen in several months was coming to town to take her out that evening. I remembered how awkward it could be to see someone you haven't seen in a long while, especially if you're a girl and it's a boy. As we chatted, I asked her if she felt nervous. She said yes. So I asked her if she would like me to pray for her. Seeing her nod, I put my arms around her and simply said, "God, you know it can be weird to see someone you haven't seen in a while. Sometimes, it's hard to think of things to talk about. I pray for Allison tonight that conversation would be natural and that they would have a good time together. Thank you, Lord. Amen."

Late that night Allison crept quietly into our room.

"Mom," she whispered with excitement, "it worked! We talked and talked, and it was fun!"

When we pray as needs arise, the spontaneity of our prayers illustrates the relevancy of our faith.

Short-range, medium-range, and long-range prayers. To keep prayer creative, have short-range, medium-range, and long-range prayers. A short-range prayer would be for the boys' homecoming dates this Saturday—that they would have fun and be kept safe. Medium-range is for wisdom for next summer's plans. Allison wants to know whether to be an intern in the church youth ministry or pursue something different. Susy's bedtime prayers recently were long-range. "Dear Lord," she prayed, "please take care of the boy I am going to marry. Help him to be getting to know You and help his parents know how to raise him right!"

I hope some children somewhere are praying for us as we raise our five!

When you toss a small rock in a pond, circles of water will radiate outward. Our prayer life will resemble this. Naturally, our greatest concerns will be those closest to us—our families. But we must not neglect praying for the next circle—our extended families, neighbors, friends. The wider circle will include those we do not know personally—believers in other lands, rulers of countries, and so on. Just as one circle of water affects the next, one small prayer may impact an entire nation. We must not underestimate the power of prayer, and we must help our children learn to pray for worldwide concerns.

The greatest privilege which we have in parenting is praying for our children. As we pray for them, it is reassuring to realize that God intimately knows each of them. There is no perfect formula for parenting. But there is power in prayer, and there is comfort in knowing that the Creator of these children has His hand on us and on them.

3. Refreshment of Fellowship

Washington's Birthday weekend was nearly here and I was very excited. Each year we spent this weekend away with our dear friends, Larry and Betsy and Bob and Elaine. Leaving children at home, we headed for the farm for our weekend of refreshment. This year Larry and Betsy were using their "frequent flyers" to fly all the way back from Japan for our time together. We would spend long hours curled up by a blazing fire talking. The guys would chop wood, and we would shop for bargains in the village.

At some point during our time, each of us would take a turn sharing what was happening in our lives personally. We would be asked tough questions: How were our marriages? Were we spending enough time with our mates? What about our relationship with a difficult child? How were we spending our money? Laughter and tears would punctuate our sharing.

We would be exhorted, held accountable, and encouraged. Mostly, we would be loved.

These relationships have been built over twenty years. They are crucial to each of us, for in order for us to become people of faith, we must have friends who will hold us accountable.

Jesus Himself had the twelve disciples, and three of those—Peter, James, and John—provided Him with a special friendship. Robert Coleman's classic book, *Master Plan of Evangelism* (Tarrytown, NY: Revell, 1963), is a beautiful portrayal of these special relationships in the life of Christ.

Recently, a prominent Christian leader succumbed to the temptation of adultery. When asked later what might have prevented this fall, he responded sadly that he wished he'd had a few close friendships with men of like faith. Only now did he realize that he needed such friends to hold him accountable for living the life God had called him to live.

When we take the time to develop close relationships with a few other believers, our children will receive two blessings.

First, they will have a set of other adults who they know love and care for them. There will be times in our children's lives when they need to hear things from an adult who is not their parent, and they will be able to go to one they know well and who cares about them.

Second, they, too, will catch the message that the Christian life is not meant to be lived alone. They will need one or two close friends of mutual encouragement, and they will naturally seek out these friends.

Bob and Elaine's daughter, Heidi, is a second-year student at the University of Virginia where Allison is in her first year. Some time ago they decided to meet together every Thursday to pray with and encourage one another. We parents did not know they were doing this until recently. How encouraging it has been for us as parents to see glimpses of answered prayers for our children!

Perhaps you desire to have a few close friends like this. God knows your desire. Simply ask Him to show you two or three people to whom you can be committed. Begin to pray for your children to develop these kinds of relationships as they grow up. God is faithful and He will answer in His time.

4. Importance of Vision

From time to time certain families come along who significantly touch the life of a nation. They seem to have imbibed from one another and their forebears a special sense of national purpose or destiny. They are people of vision who share in making an impact on many people. The descendants of Jonathan Edwards are legendary in New England. The Nehru-Ghandi family have led India for five decades until just recently, and younger Ghandis are coming along. Somewhere along the line, some parents communicated a powerful vision.

Theodore Roosevelt, Franklin Roosevelt, and Winston Churchill were all cousins. A strong vision for public service and courageous leadership was implanted in that family somewhere along the line by a family member with a sense of mission.

These diverse leaders have a message for us: we desperately need to have a vision for our families.

Vision or ambition can be a negative characteristic. It is sometimes self-seeking and ruthless. But ambition for good is desirable, and ambition to put our gifts to work for Christ is commended by Christ. In the Lord's parable about the talents, Jesus commended the ambitious servant and was clearly disgusted with the cautious one who only wanted to play it safe.

We want our children to make a significant impact on the world for the sake of Christ. How can we instill in them this sense of holy ambition? How can we help them develop a passion for a Christ-like life and a vision for their own personal ministry without "playing God" in their lives?[2]

Encouragement. Obviously as parents we must first and foremost pray for our children. Ask God to begin to show you the unique gifts He has given each child. What is his or her specific potential of which we might catch a hint? Encourage and dream with your child about the many ways in which God might use his gifts.

When Chris had his accident and was in the hospital, a young man from our church came to see him. This fifteen-year-old told Chris that when he had first heard of his accident and was praying for him, he had a strong sense that God was going to use Chris one day to lead many others to Christ, and he wanted my son to know that. Did that make an impact on Chris? You bet it did!

A sense of destiny will encourage our children. Learning to recognize their gifts will enable them to discern more clearly the ways in which God might use them.

Study your children. Is one child unusually organized? Tell her how proud you are of her ability. Encourage her to develop this gift and to use it to help others. Does one child seem to attract "hurting" peers? Is she the one who is constantly on the phone working out others' problems? Possibly she has the gift of compassion and a potential gift of counseling. She will need to know how to fine-tune these gifts and how to use them in a positive way.

One of our roles as parents is to notice the unique ways in which God has made our children and to encourage them in a positive use of their gifts. It is not our job to determine their professions. That's God's call. Ours is to notice the early stages of talents and to help our children develop them. Ultimately, these are gifts which can be used by God for the building up of His body (Ephesians 4:16).

Enrichment. Reading great biographies to our young children and encouraging them to read stories of some of the heroes of the faith will give them a sense of the way God works through His people. Schools usually have reading lists for our children. So why not parents?

Recently we asked ourselves this question and decided that we would put together a list of some of the classics of the faith which we would like for our children to read. After talking with many friends we came up with two lists—one for junior and senior high schoolers and one for collegians. Each list has ten books. We have asked our kids to complete the first list by high school graduation and the second by college graduation. As parents, we've promised to read those we haven't by the next family graduation! You will find our lists in Appendix 1.

Not only do our children need to be enriched by godly heroes through books and videos, they need to be around real, live, flesh-and-blood people.

Have believers from other countries stay in your home. Many a child's destiny has been affected by a simple dinner table conversation.

Use summers as spiritual enrichment times for your children. There is a great temptation today for kids to spend their summers earning

---

A sense of destiny will encourage our children. Learning to recognize their gifts will enable them to discern more clearly the ways in which God might use them.

---

money. While this is often legitimate, we need to ask ourselves if our child will benefit more from extra money for a new bike or from a week's stay at a Christian camp.

We have found summer to be a crucial time for our teenagers' spiritual growth. Many times our children have been enriched by exposure to different believers in situations where neither John nor I were present. Hearing biblical truths from someone else besides Mom or Dad provides tremendous reinforcement for what they learn in the family.

A couple of years ago, Allison returned home from a conference. She couldn't wait to sit her dad down and talk to him about heavy theological questions of Christian truth which she had just studied.

"Allison," he laughed, "I've been trying to teach you this for years!"

"I know, Dad," she replied. "But this was different!" (It was someone else—not just Dad!)

We must make wise use of our children's summers. Opportunities abound for spiritual enrichment, from inner-city work to mission projects and Christian camps.

When we keep encouragement and enrichment in the forefront of cultivating our family's faith, we will be using two ordinary tools to develop extraordinary people.

5. The Vitality of Worship

Occasionally, in the past, the idea of worship has drawn yawns and aroused buried memories of long, dull church services. Stiff pews, boring sermons, and squeaky choirs may have been your experience. Perhaps your faith has been fed instead by a parachurch group, a friendly Bible study in someone's home, or a retreat at a fabulous conference center.

In essence, it doesn't really matter where we receive spiritual nourishment but that we receive it. And yet there is one element that can be lacking in many groups—worship.

We have been created in the image of God, and part of this image involves a deep-seated need to worship. Throughout centuries man has created objects to worship in order to meet this need. Nearly every religion provides something or someone to worship.

Regular, corporate worship with the church family is important for each of us. God has brought the church into being as our spiritual family. The church is crosscultural, a mix of ages and interests, not limited to one social or economic standard, and the one place that ministers to us from birth to death. The church provides continuity from one generation to the next.

In today's world, it can become easy to stay at home on Sunday and rest. After all, we have a Bible study on Saturday, and our kids are at a Christian club on Monday. Do we really need church, too?

Yes, we do. We need to be meeting with the corporate body of Christ to worship and praise God. Our children need to be a part of something that includes people of all ages and backgrounds—and lasts more than a year or two.

God inhabits the praise of His people (Psalm 22:3, KJV)! Something special takes place as the body of Christ comes together weekly to praise God. Worship lifts us out of ourselves and reminds us of who God is.

But what of the child who says, "It's boring." Most children will say that at some point, but I still haven't discovered when boredom became a sin. There is nothing wrong with being bored every so often.

School gets boring, too. Yet when our child complains, we don't permit him to skip school. We know it's important. When we allow our children to skip church, but not school, we are communicating that school is more important than church.

As a child, I was expected to be in church on Sundays. Yes, I thought it often boring and a waste of my time. However, I had no choice and I went. In college I stopped attending for a time, but when I returned, I found that the old hymns and prayers which I had unconsciously memorized in my youth came back to me, bringing comfort and joy. I began to realize what I had missed by not having a special time each week just to worship.

With so many things changing in our world, there is comfort in church on Sundays where there is a familiarity of worship.

More importantly, there is a corporate sense of being part of something much greater than just those gathered in this particular building. All over the world in hundreds of languages people of all ages are meeting to worship the same God.

Worship, vision, fellowship, prayer, and God's Word are each important ingredients in growing in faith.

Becoming a family of faith is a corporate journey. We do not wait until we "arrive" and then teach our children. We will never "arrive" ourselves. Instead, as we honestly share our journey of faith with our children, we will both grow in our mutual awareness of our great need for God in our lives.

On that hot summer day in our church, our Russian friend Boris prayed for his wife and children to want to know Christ. Several months later, Jerry visited Boris and his family in Leningrad. One evening, Boris's wife came to Jerry with tears in her eyes.

"Jerry," she said in halting English, "what happened to my husband in your country? Ever since he came back he is a different person. Now he spends time with me and the children. He is kind, and He reads the Bible you gave him. I want to know, what has changed him?"

Yes, God answers our prayers for our families.

FOCUS QUESTIONS

Meditate on Psalm 111

1. Looking at this psalm, make a list of what God is like and what He has done for you.

2. What are two ways the psalmist responds to God? If you were to respond in the same way, what effect would this have on your life today?

3. What is something that you can share with one of your children that you have learned in this study? Is there a special way in which God has worked in your life?

Meditate on Ephesians 1:18–20 as a prayer, writing in the name of each child.

"My Spirit which is upon you, and
My words which I have put in your mouth,
shall not depart from your mouth, nor from the mouth
of your offspring, nor from the mouth of your offspring's off-
spring," says the LORD, "from now and forever."
(Isaiah 59:21)

JOY
(John)

NINE

*The most evident token and apparent sign
of true wisdom is a constant and unconstrained rejoicing.*

MONTAIGNE

*R*ecently, one of our sons described for me an experience he had
while riding on a New York City commuter train. As he recounted his
adventure, he described how the car had been packed with people on
their way home after a long day at work. It seemed like he was surrounded by middle-aged, pot-bellied, balding men who were worn-out.
Their clothes wrinkled and their shirts heavy with perspiration, they
hunched over in their seats or clung to the hand-holders, slouching
against one another. "They all seemed depressed," John said.

He then went on to the main point—he had met an attractive Ger-
man girl, and they had had a long, stimulating conversation on their
way to Philadelphia! But as he talked, the image of those exhausted men
stayed with me because I have often noticed the same thing. Few people
appear, from observing their faces or body language, to be happy these
days. Not that we have become overwhelmed with a national case of
depression, but as you observe people in their automobiles driving to
and from work or around town or look at people in the grocery store or
walking the malls, you see face after face that looks tired, bored, put-
out, or drained of any emotion at all. You can go for hours without
encountering a truly jolly person.

Life surely does get more serious as you become older, but even
among young people, kids don't seem to be as carefree as they were in
earlier days. It is a fact that team spirit and school enthusiasm has significantly weakened at secondary schools across the nation. High school

students are more serious than they were a few years ago and perhaps with good reason, but when you notice young people are not having as much fun, you realize that this is a symptom of a serious problem.

There are a myriad of reasons. Today many young people come from hurting, broken homes. The economy is not as promising as it was, and thus the financial future is doubtful for young people. Kids face pressure to do well academically and get into a good school that is also affordable. They are studying harder. There are scary problems in their schools; violence is commonplace. There is pressure to have sex but avoid the problem of becoming pregnant. More and more are confused about their sexual identity. The rules are changing rapidly, and many young people have no one who can compassionately and wisely help them sort it all out. No wonder it is not as much fun to be a kid these days.

One of the most important things the church can do for young people is to help them laugh. I will often peek into the room where our youth gather for evening meetings and am always encouraged to see them grinning at some goofy skit or laughing along with the leader as he shares with them the good news in ways that they can understand.

Our churches and our homes can be places of joy, and they will be if we ourselves learn the secret of joy. You might not think of joy as a character trait. You may be tempted to say that it is more a matter of personality or temperament, but my wife and I believe deeply that a spirit of joy is right at the heart of Christian moral character. It grows out of what is going on inside the person and what is going on in that person's home life.

FAITH AND JOY

A group of kids was lying contentedly on the living room floor playing a game of cards when their stern and very religious uncle came into the room and scolded them. "What a waste of time. You could be doing something beneficial, like reading the Bible."

This is not an unusual example of how some people of deep religious faith seem to be devoid of happiness. This indicates a basic misunderstanding of a fundamental principle of faith—God desires to give us good news not bad news.

The very first followers of Christ were so incredibly happy that some of the townfolk, in observing their joy one morning, thought they had been to a drinking party. You can read about it in Acts 2.

Alcohol can, in a sense, give a person a temporary sense of euphoria, help him forget his troubles, and induce a spirit of hardy enthusiasm. A

One of the most important things the church can do for young people is to help them laugh.

"happy drunk" feels no pain. His world is, for the moment, a wonderful place. It doesn't last very long, and eventually the body reacts rather unpleasantly. Sooner or later, the night-before catches up with the morning-after, and the one who was so carefree is overcome with regret. But while the experience lasts, the people can't help but notice his carefree gaiety.

According to the New Testament, that must have been something akin to what characterized those sober but joyful believers on the day of Pentecost. That morning they were caught up in the joyful presence of God Almighty and the sheer delight of being alive to God's Spirit. God desires no less for each of us.

There have always been Christians who had this kind of joy. St. Francis and his band of Franciscans had to be reproved in church because they were so happy when they were worshipping God. The early Methodists were criticized by the more formal church people for being "too enthusiastic." The Methodists even took some of their hymn tunes from the opera. They turned popular dance tunes into songs of praise for God. General Booth of the Salvation Army did the same thing. He told people that when they felt the Spirit, they could leap up during the worship and during the prayers. There is a story about a formal musician who was attending one of the Salvation Army gatherings and was quite offended by their enthusiasm. As the story goes, he appealed to the drummer not to hit the drums so hard. To which the drummer said, "Oh, sir, I'm so happy I could burst the blessed drum." Then he went over to a man who was playing the French horn and he said the same thing. The man said, "But, sir, I'm so full of joy, I want to blow this thing quite straight."[1]

When a person really grasps the good news that God is real, that God knows and loves us each individually, and that He has given the ultimate gift so that we might know Him, know His caring guidance, and know we have eternal life, a sense of joy begins to develop deep inside. If our minds and hearts have been touched by God's kindness, and we nurture our souls on a diet of the grace and goodness of God, joyfulness will result. People express it in different ways, depending on their temperament or personality. Not everyone is as joyously effusive as that horn blower, but a strong faith in a wonderful, gracious God is a powerful incentive toward a joyous spirit.

Children seem to be born with a natural and joyous sense of wonder at the world around them and toward God. If we can stimulate and encourage that sense of wonder when they are young, it will sustain them through the years. A sense of awe brings peace and joy within. The wonder of Almighty God creating this world around us and then creating each of us so uniquely different is strongly appealing to little ones. As we help them notice the wonder of caterpillars and butterflies, a bulb growing into brilliant flowers, of snowflakes and ant hills, this nurtures a sense of anticipation at the diversity of God's world and God's people. *There is no time for boredom for the person who has been nurtured in the wonders of God.* It's an attitude that stays with us for life.

Sometimes it seems that the creatures that God made have this sense of this joy and wonder, too. When I take Duchess, our retriever, out for her early morning outing, she seems overcome with joy at the day itself. She will just sit and look up at the sky and trees, blissfully peaceful. Then she will throw herself down on the grass and roll and roll, just for the sheer enjoyment of how good it feels. I never cease to wonder at this sense of freedom and delight, and she helps me to recover some of the same sense of joy as I, too, am reminded of how beautiful is the world God created.

Joy is a natural response to so much that is good in the world—if we have eyes to see it.

When I was in college, one of my best friends was Larry Roadman, an all-star Lacrosse player. He used to greet me walking across campus with the words, "Rejoice, Yates!"

Sometimes I found this irritating, especially since we usually met early in the morning before an eight o'clock class. I was tired, concerned about my studies and the mess our country was in with Vietnam and

---

A sense of awe brings peace and joy within. The wonder of Almighty God creating this world around us and then creating each of us so uniquely different is strongly appealing to little ones.

L. B. J. How could I rejoice? But he was right, and I was wrong. The person who knows God is called to be a rejoicing person in at least some way at all times.

Seventy times in the New Testament we are told to rejoice. This was a word commonly used by early Christians as both a greeting and a farewell, both in speech and in writing. It was even used in drinking a toast.

Jesus in speaking to the disciples said, "These things I have spoken to you, that My joy may be in you, and that your joy may be made full" (John 15:11).

"Your sorrow," He said, "will be turned to joy" (John 16:20).

"Ask," He said, "and you will receive, that your joy may be made full" (John 16:24).

His prayer for all disciples and for us was "that they may have My joy made full in themselves" (John 17:13).

What is this joy which G. K. Chesterton called "the gigantic secret of the Christian?" Joy is something too great to be confused with the superficial emotion we call happiness. Joy is not transitory, not dependent upon the weather, events, or other people. Joy is not something one can achieve for oneself. It cannot be accomplished by filling some formula and is more than simply one's temperament. Joy is an emotion, but it is also much more. We are well off, all our loved ones are happy, people like us, life is smiling at us. Then we experience what we call happiness, which is a wonderful thing. But joy is deeper.

Joy is contentment and a sense of gladness or well-being deep inside the core of a person. It is closely related to peace. Joy is slightly more active; it is peace that is smiling. Peace is contentment, but joy is contentment that is cheerfully, actively approaching life. This does not mean that we are to go around grinning all the time, although it probably would do us some good. I have read that laughter has a profound and instantaneous effect on virtually every important organ in the human body. Laughter reduces tensions and relaxes the tissues as well as exercising most of the vital organs. Laughter, even when forced, results in a healthy effect on us both mentally and physically.

In his book, *Screwtape Letters*, C. S. Lewis pictures the devil musing on this whole phenomenon of Christian joy and laughter.

> What the real cause is we do not know. Something like it is expressed in much of the detestable art which the humans call music, and something like it occurs in Heaven. It does us [demons] no good and should always be discouraged. Besides, the phenomenon is of itself disgusting and a direct insult to the realism, dignity, and austerity of hell.[2]

I suppose the enemy does feel that way. Joy is a gift God offers us; we cannot produce it. We receive it as we trust in God. The opposite of joy is not unhappiness but unbelief, a lack of trust in God. Joy is the attitude that says something like this:

> I am going to approach life with the certainty that this is God's world. He has made it and me for His purposes. I am going to do what I can to serve Him and serve others. Where I fail, or where I encounter pain or sadness or evil that I cannot overturn myself, I will hope in God that He will ultimately bring about His own good purposes.

WHERE DOES JOY COME FROM?

In a sense, joy is a result of life that is lived according to the seven principles my wife and I have described thus far in this book. As we mentioned in the introduction, character is demonstrated by living a life consistent with clearly held principles. We have looked at integrity, teachability, self-discipline, compassion, servanthood, courage, and faith. A life built upon these principles will not be without trouble, for no one can promise that. Christ certainly did not. Tragedy, pain, and disappointment are unavoidable parts of life, but they need not destroy our inner sense of joy. Joy goes deeper than these things. A person who is committed to these seven principles, who seeks to live this way day-in and day-out, even though he may often fall short and fail, will experience some sense of inner peace and satisfaction. Joy comes from knowing who you are and who God is in relationship to yourself and knowing how God wants you to conduct yourself. A quiet joy comes when we live the way God calls us to live.

Think of it this way. If you are convinced in your heart that there is a good and productive way to live and relate to others and give yourself to living that way, you have a sense of present satisfaction that you are doing with your life what you ought to be doing. That, in itself, is no guarantee of happiness, but it does give a sense of personal inner harmony which is joy. No one ever fully lives the life he or she desires, but to know that you are striving to live consistently with your principles gives you this contentment. Living in total inconsistency with one's principles produces the opposite: dissatisfaction, disappointment, and discontent.

However, even the most principled person may not always experience a joyful spirit; there is more to a joyful life than moral consistency. We have observed at least three habits or disciplines that have a direct impact upon our ability to become more joyful people. They grow out of the seven principles we have been considering and are daily habits which, as they are cultivated, actually enhance our sense of joy.

1. An Attitude of Gratitude

First is the habit of thankfulness. A thankful heart produces a joyful spirit. People who focus on their difficulties are difficult to be around. People who focus on their blessings are a blessing to be around. *Gratitude* is the ground out of which a joyful, peaceful spirit can grow. All of us have much for which we can be grateful, but do we realize it? And do we give expression to it? Often our tendency is to focus on our problems rather than on our blessings, and since we all have plenty of problems, we have ample opportunity to become discouraged.

Life is difficult. You may have problems with your health or with one of your children. Perhaps your best friend has just declared bankruptcy. Your neighbor struggles with in-law problems. We all have problems. Jesus said, "In the world you will have trouble" (John 16:33, NIV). This can cause discouragement.

There is a story that the devil was having a yard sale one day, and many of his tools were on display. They were a fiendish lot, each priced according to its value. There was hatred and jealousy, deceit, lying, and pride, but over to the side was the most well-worn of all of his tools and his most valuable. That tool was discouragement. When asked why, the devil said, "It is more useful than any other. When I can't bring down one of my victims with any of the rest of these tools, I can always count on this one. So few people realize that it belongs to me."

Discouragement—enemy of joy. Discouragement is the enemy of joy that causes one to want to quit—to say, "what's the use," and throw in the towel. If we are going to live productive lives, we have got to learn to overcome discouragement. In a sense, the more discouragement a person can overcome, the greater the person is.

A man who many believe was the greatest American president is a good example. At seven years of age, his family was forced out of their home and he went to work. When he was nine, his mother died. He lost his job as a store clerk when he was twenty-two. He wanted to go to law school but did not have the education. At age twenty-three, he went into debt to be a partner in a small store. Three years later, the business partner died, and the resulting huge debt took years to repay. When he was twenty-eight after courting a girl for four years, he asked her to marry him, and she said no. At thirty-seven, on his third try, he was elected to Congress but then failed to be reelected. A son was born to him that year, but four years later the son died. When he was forty-five, he ran for the Senate but lost. At age forty-seven, he sought the vice presidency of the United States and lost. Two years later, he ran for the Senate and lost again. But at age fifty-one, he was elected president of the United States. Abraham Lincoln was a man who learned to face discouragement and move beyond it. We must do the same.

Persons of every age have problems. Young people may not like their face or their figure, their friends or their grades. They may not succeed in sports or get the part they want in the school play. A few years later, their problems will be different. There is not enough money, or the job is not what you expected. Alcoholism or divorce trouble you. Many people are unable to have children. Each of us will lose loved ones through death, and so it goes. Sadness, loneliness, and disappointment confront all of us.

Three options. There are three options for dealing with discouragement. The first is simply to *give in to it*—let it overwhelm you and eat at you as you focus on the negative, become depressed, bitter, and hopeless. Many people elect this option. Recently when one young person in Maine committed suicide, thirty-three more children attempted to take their lives as well. There are thousands of teen suicides in the United States annually as kids give in to their discouragement.

This is a big temptation. The disappointments keep coming and just when you see light at the end of the tunnel you realize it is another train coming at you full speed ahead.

A second option is to *deny the problem.*

- "My husband doesn't really have a drinking problem."
- "This sickness really is nothing serious."
- "My daughter's loneliness really is not something to worry about."

There are two ways people of all ages tend to deny problems. Either we minimize them—"I know we are in debt but something will work out," or "I have lost my job. Sooner or later somebody's going to appreciate me."

Or our denial can take the form of spiritualizing the problem—"My wife is so sad. We haven't been able to have children for these twelve years of our marriage but it's okay—praise God!"

If there is a problem in your life, you usually don't help yourself by denying it. If there is a problem in your marriage, if you haven't been sleeping together or talking to one another, if there is coldness or desperation setting in, it will help no one if you deny it, minimize it, or spiritualize it. Neither does it help our children if we encourage them to deny serious problems that they face.

Instead of giving in to the problem or denying it, a third option provides a better way. We must *deal with discouraging situations by facing them with realism and faith.*

Our children need to learn to analyze their big problems and ask, "Is there anything I can do to deal with this difficulty? If there is, I will do it." Let's help them think it through for themselves and determine what their options are.

But we do them no favors by pretending that every problem has a solution. Sometimes accepting that there is nothing to be done and determining to move ahead in other areas as we live with this problem is the best solution. In that case, we have the opportunity to teach our child to make a decision to trust God in spite of the problem. The psalmist caught this spirit when he wrote, "The LORD reigns; let the earth rejoice" (Psalm 97:1).

As long as God rules, I can be joyful in trusting that eventually His good will prevail. God is *over* all things; He is not *responsible* for all things but has promised to work through all things and bring good to those who trust Him. God can use the worst developments to bring about the best ends.

The story was told once about a ship that wrecked. The only survivor washed up exhausted on a small, uninhabited island. He cried to God to save him and daily watched the horizon for help. Finally he managed to build a rough hut to protect his few articles. One day after searching for food, he was stung with grief to see his hut consumed in flames. The worst had happened. What an answer to his prayer! But early the next day a ship drew in to rescue him. "How did you know I was here?" the man said. The reply: "We saw your smoke signal."

Tell your children stories of how you have experienced God's help in your own life when you have been in turmoil. This is terrifically encouraging to them. When our children begin to see how God can bring them through and beyond discouraging circumstances, then they can begin to thank God even in the midst of difficult times. This cultivates the attitude of gratitude that produces a joyful spirit. When your child has a difficult time, sympathize and be understanding, but help him remember some of the good things as well.

Matthew Henry, the famous scholar, was once attacked by thieves and robbed of his purse. He wrote these words in his diary: "Let me be thankful first because I was never robbed before. Second, because although they took my purse, they did not take my life. Third, because although they took my all, it was not much. And fourth, because it was I who was robbed and not I who robbed."[3]

2. An Attitude of Worship

In the latter part of the twentieth century there has been something of a recovery of worship. Many people have begun to discover that simply believing and seeking to faithfully follow the Lord is not enough to bring satisfaction to one's soul. Many of the churches that have emphasized the importance of liturgical worship have found young people streaming in to them because they are hungry for a taste of God's awesome majesty. This sense of the transcendence and greatness of God is sometimes lost in informal worship. The older liturgical forms at times

Tell your children stories of how you have experienced God's help in your own life when you have been in turmoil. This is terrifically encouraging to them.

seem to capture God's holiness and satisfy something deep inside of us. Being reminded of the greatness of God, His power, His sovereign might and glorious purposes strengthens our inner sense of peace. Sometimes God touches us most profoundly in worship.

Real worship occurs when we pull away from distractions in order to be still and know the reality and presence of God. It occurs when we consciously aim ourselves—mind, body, soul, and spirit—toward almighty God, when we reflect upon who He is and what He has done for us. We worship when we pray, when we confess our sins, commit ourselves to Him, and ask His help for our lives and for others. You can worship when you are alone in the middle of a forest and when you are among a congregation of one thousand people. It should happen both places but does not always happen when it is supposed to.

When I was about nine or ten, I took my best friend to church with me one Sunday. I don't know how much he went to church, and certainly he didn't go to an Episcopal church like we did. We went to the solemn, early morning Communion service without any music. The words were ancient, and the prayers seemed to go on for about an hour and a half. I remember Joe at some point about halfway through the service on his knees slumped over the kneeling rail looking at me with an amazing expression on his face. His face was pale white, drained of all color, and he looked like he was about to faint. He didn't say anything but the expression said, *Why on earth are we doing this?* At that age, I don't think I could have articulated a coherent answer, but I now realize there are at least five simple reasons.

First, God's people have always been led by God to worship Him. From the Garden of Eden through the book of Revelation, the people of God have built their lives around worship and taught their children to worship God as well. In the book of Exodus, one chapter is devoted to the Ten Commandments and then forty-four chapters devoted to worship. What was the great sin of Israel? Idolatry—when they didn't worship God.

When God became a man, how did wise, believing people respond to Him? Three wise men came into the house and saw the child and fell down and worshiped Him. And that's the way it was throughout Jesus' life for all who realized who He was. The Gospels describe sick people worshiping Him, His disciples worshiping Him, a synagogue official worshiping Him. On and on it goes. When God took His Son back into heaven, His followers continued to meet and worship Him. Every Sabbath they met to worship.

The *second* reason worship is important is that it reminds us of the most important things in life—who God is, what He is like, what He promises and expects of us.

Third, worship when it occurs as God wants it, quiets us, and enables us to renew our relationship with God. J. B. Phillips said, "If the Christian is to maintain his spiritual life within him, he must . . . elbow a space in his daily activities when he can obey the command to 'be still and know that I am God.' "

Worship quiets us and enables us to know God. Worship has the potential to produce a unique moment of stillness in God's presence where joy steals across our spirits.

Thomas Carlisle, the English poet, defined *worship* as a "transcendent wonder." In one moment together, quiet and still before God, we can in a sense touch eternity. There is a momentary timelessness when sometimes, as the hymnwriter says, we are "lost in wonder."

Fourth, worship strengthens our resolve to be Christ's man or woman.

And *fifth,* worship helps us to become more fully developed by God into the man or woman He has created us to be, like a flower unfolding before the sun in the springtime. As the hymn says, "hearts unfold like flowers before thee praising thee their Son above."[4]

Because freedom of worship is vital to a person's health, it is a terrible thing for oppressive governments to forbid it. One of the great Russian literary giants, Feodor Dostoevsky, said it most perfectly.

> The one essential condition of human existence is that man should always be able to bow down before something infinitely great. If men are deprived of the infinitely great, they will not go on living and will die of despair. The infinite and the eternal are as essential for man as the little planet on which he dwells.

Jesus said that God actively seeks people to worship Him. Why? Is God so insecure that He needs people to tell Him how great He is? No. God knows how important worship is to our very existence. Worship is to the spiritual, moral life what physical exercise is to the body. Our souls atrophy without worship. Worship feeds the joy within. We have a responsibility to make a firm commitment to worship and to teach our children to worship as well.

We do this by praying with them, as well as by taking them to church. We do it by pointing out God's great gifts in our lives and thanking Him consistently together, spontaneously as well as at mealtimes and other regular times. We teach them also through music as we take advantage of the many music tapes that are now available for children and adults aimed at helping us grow in our ability to praise God. Teaching our children songs of praise and worship gives them the materials so that they can express their thanks to God. We often listen to these tapes on a Sunday morning getting ready for church or in the car or when we are traveling together. Sometimes when we are lying on a blanket out in the pasture at night looking at the stars, we will sing songs of thanksgiving to God together. Sometimes while at family prayer, at mealtimes, or bedtimes, we will limit our prayers to prayers of thankfulness to God for blessings or praise to God for His different characteristics that cause us to love Him. Worship like this is not painful or burdensome; it is a most normal, natural response to the goodness of God. But we must make time to do it.

3. An Attitude with Eternal Perspective

A joyful spirit is related to our perspective on the here and now and how it relates to eternity. Perhaps the most important gift we can give our children is the awareness that this life is simply the launching pad for the larger life we enter at death. This life is a first step of a journey that is forever.

To put it into the words of Paul, "our citizenship is in heaven" (Philippians 3:20). Even though we live here on earth in our own culture, we are part of something much bigger.

When my oldest daughter and I spent some time in Africa a few years ago, we visited numerous remote villages in the mountains of Kenya. I will never forget the reaction of the small children in one little village as we drove up in our clergyman friend's tiny and ancient Datsun. Dozens of little children came racing up to see us and looked at us as if my daughter and I were aliens from some other planet. Later that day, the schoolmaster explained that we were in fact the first white folks that the little ones had ever seen. It was an unusual feeling, especially when our meeting and presentation to them was all over and the schoolmaster had presented us with a lively, noisy, clucking rooster as a thank-you gift to bring back to our family here in the States! We felt somewhat out of place there, like aliens—present but not totally belonging because our home was elsewhere.

Perhaps some of your friends are residents in our country but not citizens. For a person to change his citizenship is a major decision. My sister is married to an Englishman. They live in England, and he is a citizen of the U.K., but she is maintaining her American citizenship. To change one's citizenship is to decide once and for all that this place, which has been my home all my life, is no longer going to be my home, and my loyalty is no longer to this nation but to another. Many people make the decision to live and die in our country but are not able to change their citizenship. They work here, spend time here, earn their living here, but this is not their home. Their home is in a far country because that is the way it must be.

The supreme reason why Jesus was so different from all other people, apart from His divinity, was that He was always conscious of the fact that this world was not really His home. He chose to make this His home for a while, but He never lost sight of the knowledge that He had come forth from God and was going back. He was like a pilgrim—just passing through for a while. He was living in this world by the values and with the perspective of heaven. What was true of Jesus also becomes true of those who follow Him.

We live on the earth, we breathe its air, we enjoy its beauty, we are responsible to take care of it, we are bound by the Earth's laws. We love our earthly home. It is a beautiful, wonderful, blessed place of temporary

---

Perhaps the most important gift we can give our children is the awareness that this life is simply the launching pad for the larger life we enter at death. This life is a first step of a journey that is forever.

---

residence, but only the first step toward something so much grander and greater and bigger and more overwhelming. Life on earth is like hors d'oeuvres before the real feast to come.

When we make the decision that our love for God is going to take precedence over any other commitment in our lives, and we realize that heaven is our ultimate home, this affects the way we see ourselves, what we value most, and also how we see our circumstances. All three of these viewpoints produce a deeper sense of joy.

The person who follows Christ has a new identity and sees himself differently. There are scores of ways in which we might identify ourselves. This person may be a nurse or a businessman, attorney, diplomat, carpenter, plumber, or student. Or you might be a Californian or Washingtonian or an Englishman. But what really matters is that I am Christ's person; this is my ultimate identity.

This gives me great joy, because, first, it means I am valuable to God. We know how naturally selfish we are as human beings. We know that we have done the things we ought not to have done, and we have left undone those things we ought to have done. We have apologized sincerely to God, and through Christ, God has forgiven us. We have become God's children by faith. Every day we can remind ourselves and our children that we belong to Christ.

You may be young and full of health and vigor, or you may be old and tired; your body may be weak and your skin quietly going "wrink, wrink, wrink" every day. You may be losing your attractiveness; you may be a success or a failure. In reality, however, these are only minor factors in how we see ourselves because first and last we are Christ's—this is our identity.

Second, this eternal perspective affects what we value most. When we follow Christ, our values become God's values rather than society's values. The values of heaven turn the values of earth upside-down (this is what the Bible means when it says the streets of heaven are paved with gold—what's most valuable on earth is only good for paving streets in heaven).

If people believe that this life is all that there is and that when you are dead you are dead, then it is easy to understand why they feel that they must run as hard as they can and see as much as they can and experience every sensation possible. They feel they must have the nicest, best equipment, the most comfortable home, the latest in labor-saving appliances, the newest gadgets, the most time-saving devices, the most comfortable car, furniture, the nicest wardrobe, the most exciting vacation. They must see every show, sample every dish, check out every new philosophy. If you think this body is the only one you are ever going to have, then you will do everything you can to make it last as long as possible, look as good as it can, and smell as nice as it can. But if you know that it is only a temporary place of residence, then when it begins to wind down and wear out, you will not be quite so discouraged.

This leads to the third way an eternal perspective affects the way in which we live and raise our children. The things that are most difficult, discouraging, and troublesome for us now, when seen from the perspective of eternity, have a way of becoming less important. If your child falls and scrapes her knee, she may cry as though the biggest tragedy has befallen her. From the perspective of an adult, her father knows that this slight accident is nowhere near as catastrophic as the child thinks it is. He has a more mature perspective. This does not mean he is any less sympathetic with the child, but he knows that in a very short while this problem will be safely in the past. One who has the perspective of eternity in mind is able to view life's momentary difficulties with more peace and contentment. However difficult things may be, we know that the time is coming when they will be unimportant. This enables us to maintain a spirit of peace and joy.

As we look beyond this life to the next, we are all the more challenged to give of ourselves in this life, for this is what God calls us to do. Knowing our ultimate destination enables us to live out this present life with a greater sense of commitment, abandon, and peacefulness. We love the good things of this world and are pursuing God's work, pouring ourselves out in service to one another as though each person we meet were Christ Himself. But we are not deceived by this world's values. We are not misled that this here-and-now is all there is. This life and this world is just a beginning. We make of it all we can for God's sake, but heaven is our home.

This life is just the cover, the title page, and the preface of the book God is writing about you throughout eternity. When you enter into the next life, you are going to begin chapter one of the great book that God will write and keep on writing forever.

Joy and peace may come more naturally to some than to others, but they are in fact a part of our birthright as believers. They take root deep within the soul of a person who builds his life upon the goodness and guidance of God. Joy is not always smiling or laughing, though often it is. But joy is the fruit of *choosing* to trust in God's adequacy to meet our needs, *choosing* to abide by the eternal principles He has given us in Christ, *choosing* to thank and worship Him as a consistent habit, and *seeking* always to view circumstances from the long perspective of eternity rather than the short perspective of the here and now.

FOCUS QUESTIONS

Meditate on Luke 12:22–34

1. Consider the wisdom of these words of Jesus, and praise God for those rich promises. Are you a person for whom laughter comes easily and often? Are you contented deep down inside most of the time? Are you a joyful Christian?

2. You have read that inner joy is often connected to (a) a spirit of gratefulness, (b) the habit of worship, (c) keeping the eternal perspective. Of these three is there one area in particular for which you need to ask God's help?

3. Are you prone to focusing on discouraging things rather than on blessings? Can you think of examples? How might you right now see one situation from God's perspective?

Meditate on Romans 8:18–39, thanking God especially for His promises in verses 28–39.

> *Beloved, now we are children of God,*
> *and it has not appeared as yet what we shall be.*
> *We know that, when He appears, we shall be like Him,*
> *because we shall see Him just as He is. And every one who has*
> *this hope fixed on Him purifies himself, just as He is pure.*
> *(1 John 3:2–3)*

THE HOME WHERE CHARACTER BLOSSOMS

TEN

(Susan)

No man ever sank under the burden of the day.
It is when tomorrow's burden is added to the burden
of today that the weight is more than a man can bear.
Never load yourself so. If you find yourself so loaded, at least
remember this: it is your own doing, not God's. He begs you to
leave the future to Him, and mind the present.

GEORGE MACDONALD

*A*deep blue sky laced with soft white clouds arches as a fitting canopy over the gorgeous garden. Everywhere bright colors reach upward as dozens of different flowers cover the hillside. Deep purple iris rest alongside bright pink poppies. Nestled nearby are violets and fading forget-me-nots. Peonies with blossoms as big as your hand seem to beckon you forward down a lovely path trimmed with liriope. Coral bells stir in the gentle breezes, waving their deep-red flower stalks at you. Mockingbirds sing a symphony of love songs just for you. And sweet garden scents make you feel so good, you just want to hug somebody. It's indeed one of those perfect spring days.

A contented sigh escapes the lips of the gardener. There's pleasure in his eyes and a smile across his tanned, wrinkled face. Not wanting to break the spell of wonder, he is completely still as he takes in the beauty before him. A sense of awe overcomes him as he lets his eyes rove from plant to plant. He feels a special kinship with each one for he has carefully chosen and nurtured it. He has even placed it in just the spot that will enhance its own loveliness and yet contribute to the beauty of the whole garden. Its beauty is now his delight.

THE INTENT OF THE GARDENER

When the gardener first began to prepare this lovely garden, he knew that he wanted to create a thing of beauty. He expected his efforts to bring joy to all who would come in contact with it, and he delighted in his task. His garden would reflect the glory of the Creator and cause people to consider His goodness. Yes, there would be difficulties and disappointments, but he was not daunted. The fruit of his labors was well worth the task.

Our families can be likened to this garden. God wants them to be full of love and beauty, a refuge of security where there is an appreciation of one another. He expects good things to happen in our families, for He created our families to be as the French say, "La petite église," the little church. Our family represents the union of Christ and us with the Father. "For where two or three come together in my name, there am I with them" (Matthew 18:20, NIV).

Of course there will be difficulties and disappointments for families on earth, but God will be there in the midst of trouble.

And as our families seek Him, He will be found, and He will use our families to reflect His faithfulness.

THE MAKEUP OF THE GARDEN

A grin spreads across the old gardener's face as he notices one particularly beautiful flower. It had taken him a long time to decide what he should plant in this special area. There was a huge jagged rock and a curious bend in the path. A very special plant was needed to make the rock look like it had been intentionally placed at this very spot as a work of art. Yes, the soft pink of the lovely old sweetheart rose climbing over the rough edges of the rock makes it look like it springs right from Monet's canvas. Diversity has indeed produced a lovely harmony. He is pleased with his choices.

When God looks at our families, He is delighted for He has carefully chosen each member to be in this specific family. He has created each person with unique gifts and distinct personalities. No two are

---

When the gardener first began to prepare this lovely garden, he knew that he wanted to create a thing of beauty. He expected his efforts to bring joy to all who would come in contact with it, and he delighted in his task.

---

alike. Sometimes the differences in nature will be irritating and cause discord. And yet as we recognize the differences as potential blessings, we will learn how they actually strengthen the family.

Twin boys age four look exactly alike, yet God has given them different natures. On a walk with their mom, one son lags far behind. Carefully he notices every rock, occasionally overturning one in search of a hidden worm. Bits of paper or discarded cans become rare treasures to bring to his mother. A peaceful soul, he walks as if in a daze, so occupied is he with his surroundings. His pace is slow, as if he had not a care in the world. Way ahead, his brother races, calling out to people passing by. Back and forth he runs to his mother with ideas bursting forth. "Mom, can we go to the park next?" Or "let's get the bikes out." Or "I want to build a tree house in the old oak tree." The frazzled Mom calls to one, "hurry up" and to the other "slow down."

Yet in God's perfect wisdom, He has created two distinct individuals with gifts for this family. One son will teach the family to slow down, to wonder at the world, to take in God's creation, and to appreciate life. He will bring peace and enable others to relax. The other son will stimulate ideas. He will cause the family to plan ahead. He will have visions for tomorrow. His energy will infuse those around him.

Certainly there will be times of frustration for the parents as they balance these personalities and seek to bring out the best of both. But they will be encouraged when they remember that God is at work in their family, allowing the diversity of its members to create a lovely harmony. God has chosen our family members, and He makes no mistakes.

INTRUDERS IN THE GARDEN

Bending down, the gardener peers closely at the leaves of the little green and gold hosta. A look of concern casts a shadow over his twinkling eyes.

"It's those blasted slugs again," he sighs.

There's always something trying to invade his garden. Last month it was the spring's first crop of aphids that caused him problems. Before that, the squirrels tried to dig up his bulbs. Once some persistent moles caused a lot of damage but he learned how to trap them, and now he knows what to do if they reappear.

Some of the intruders to his garden have been dangerous for his young plants, but others, though unsightly, have actually benefited it. The praying mantises are, oh, so ugly and have frightened a child or two, but they have actually helped by feasting on the aphids and white flies that come every year.

With the wisdom born of experience, the old gardener knows how to handle these pesky intruders. He also knows that there will always be surprise invaders—both helpful and harmful—into his garden. He must stay alert for both. And he must respond to them in a way which will strengthen his garden.

Into each of our families will come intruders. An illness, a job loss, an unwanted move, a rebellious child, a financial difficulty are but a few of the common invaders in most households. Some will be more obvious than others. As parents, our job is to recognize the intruders and to respond appropriately. An unwanted intruder can become a means for building strong character.

A young couple with two children had lived on the upper edge of wealth. A fine home in the best section of town, fancy cars, full-time household help, the best private schools, and exotic vacations seemed routine for this family. But a financial crisis appeared through no fault of the husband. The economy took an unexpected turn for the worse, and his business collapsed, leaving the family in financial ruin. The house was sold, and the family moved into a rental home and enrolled their kids in public schools. There was no longer any household help.

An unwelcome intruder? Yes. A devastating blow to the family? Yes. But a strengthening experience for this family? Yes. These wise parents knew that although much had been taken away, they still had each other. And they knew that God was still in control. They began to pray for God to use this mess for good in their family. With no household help to do the chores, the husband and wife began to work together. The kids learned how to help new ways. New conversations took place. Compassion blossomed, and a sense of unity developed. Depending upon themselves for entertainment, the family found pleasure in simple things. And they began to sense that some things which had seemed to be so important weren't really so crucial after all.

Certainly there were incredibly difficult adjustments, but alongside the pain, fresh values began to blossom. In dealing with this unwanted invader, the parents thrust themselves on their heavenly Father and on one another.

In the process, they discovered that an undesirable intruder became a means to achieving a deeper harmony within their family.

SEASONS IN THE GARDEN

Sweat begins to trickle down the neck of the gardener as the sun climbs higher in the sky. Irritating gnats nip at his ears, and he swats at them with an attitude of resignation.

"Yep, it's gonna be a hot one today," he mumbles to himself.

"But that warmth sure does feel good to my bones," he reminds himself.

For he is truly glad that spring is here. Of all the seasons, he loves this one the best. His friend up the road, also a gardener, loves the fall best. Crisp nights, hints of frost, the soft yellow chrysanthemums, and the pale blue of the fall asters are more enjoyable to his neighbor.

"Fall's okay," he reckons, "but spring is truly delightful."

As he considers the seasons, he is reminded that each one has its challenges and its blessings for gardeners.

Winter brings the challenge of boredom and the occasional depression caused by a succession of bleak, cold, gray days. However, there is the blessing of some rest. It's a time for reflection and planning. From these quiet hours come rejuvenation and new dreams for the spring.

Spring brings with it the challenge of the late frost that will kill young shoots. He must watch the weather carefully and be ready to protect the young plants with mulch or burlap. A threat of drought can also make things difficult for his developing plants. On the other hand, there's the tremendous blessing of seeing that first tiny shoot peek through the black dirt, that delicate bud begin to uncurl its velvet petals.

Family life has seasons, too. Indeed, all of life has seasons. There's the season of being a collegian, a single working adult, newlyweds, parents of toddlers, parents of teens, and the season of the "golden years."

Every season will have specific challenges and unique blessings. It is important to articulate the challenges but to focus on the blessings.

Having five children in seven years made our season of small children definitely challenging. When the twins (numbers four and five in the family lineup) were six weeks old, we moved to Virginia. We didn't know anyone, and we had no family nearby. John had his first job as the senior minister of a church.

For the first several months we lived in our new home, our kitchen was gutted for renovation. I remember doing dishes in the bathroom sink and eating cold cuts because the stove was on the porch. When the kitchen was finally finished, a severe storm hit, causing a huge tree to fall through the roof of my new kitchen. Construction had to begin all over again!

Since I was nursing the colicky twins, those early days required a monumental effort in order for me to make it until nap time. I often felt that my brain had stopped working. Twice in one week I went grocery shopping and arrived home only to realize that I had forgotten to bring the groceries home from the store!

One of the biggest challenges for me was that I felt that I was not accomplishing anything. Clean kids got dirty almost immediately, a neat house lasted only through naptime, and dinner was a far cry from a gourmet meal. Accustomed to accomplishments and measurable goals, I quickly became frustrated. Oh, I knew in my head that what I was doing was important, but my spirit wasn't feeling it. There wasn't instant satisfaction.

Toddlers make mothers feel they have lost control of their families. They give orders like generals! They are unpredictable and into everything. It's their season of discovery.

As I spoke with other mothers of young children, I discovered that they, too, were experiencing similar frustrations. Simply knowing that I wasn't alone gave me great comfort. But most importantly, I began to identify the challenges and yet focus on the blessings.

Toddlers make mothers feel they have lost control of their families. They give orders like generals! They are unpredictable and into everything. It's their season of discovery. Although at times irritating, these children can remind us to become observers ourselves and herein is a blessing. Observe the funny things they say and write them down, for their humorous innocence lasts only for a short time.

At her first view of the ocean, Libby said, "It's too full, Mommy! I think we ought to let some of it out."

When asked what Superman does, Chris responded, "He flies in the sky talking to Jesus and God."

Writing down these funny things the little ones said was one way I learned to focus on the blessings of the season instead of feeling overwhelmed by the challenges.[1]

Now we are into the teen years. I love this season. Just as one gardener enjoyed fall and the other spring, different seasons in life will affect people differently. But every season has challenges and blessings, and we are most enriched when we choose to focus on the blessings.

THE ATMOSPHERE OF THE GARDEN

"What a smart little plant you are to produce such a lovely flower," the gardener compliments the foxglove. And then he notices a small, late-blooming columbine whose growth has been overshadowed by the larger plant.

"Well, little one, you look as if you need some more sunlight."

Gently he moves the smaller plant over just a bit so it, too, will be in the full sun. He has a special place in his heart for late bloomers, perhaps because he had been one himself.

Continuing along the path, he speaks to his plants, coaxing them along and praising them. Here and there he notices a specific need and sets about making necessary adjustments. He knows there will never be perfection in his garden; there will always be a plant behind in its growth or one that is fading. Some plants need more care than others, and some need more care in different seasons. Yet he loves this place, and he would never neglect any of his plants.

So intent is he on his job that he hardly notices the sun is beginning to set. He has had such a lovely day working with his plants that he hasn't thought about the time. He feels so at home here among his friends. He knows his work will never end; there will always be more to do. Quite honestly, he would be lost if his work were ever finished. But because he is a true gardener, his joy is in the work.

Glancing one more time at the vast beauty before him, and taking a deep smell of the varied fragrances, he turns toward home knowing that tomorrow he will return to this joyful atmosphere.

In the joyful atmosphere of a home, character will blossom. Our home can be a happy refuge or a depressing stopover. God's design is for it to be a place full of joy. That doesn't mean a house where people put on an "everything's wonderful, aren't we perfect" act. Plastic flowers would ruin the garden; they aren't genuine. Natural flowers create the beauty of the garden. Our home is to be a place where we are genuine— free to be ourselves, natural, without pretense. A home where people with weaknesses and strengths live together, encouraging, forgiving, and picking one another up.

A home should be full of joy springing from large doses of love and great amounts of forgiveness. "Love covers a multitude of sins" (1 Peter 4:8). And it's a good thing, because in our home live sinful people needing lots of love.

Love is communicated in different ways—a simple word of encouragement, hugging and comforting a disappointed child, a mother greeting you at the door with gladness that you are home from school or work. Maybe it's a quick phone call from the office simply to say, "Honey, I just wanted to say I love you," or a note in a child's lunch box saying, "I'm glad you're mine. I love you." It's Dad offering to fix dinner while Mom curls up with a book. Love is communicated in asking forgiveness when you say a hurtful thing and in forgiving another even when you don't feel like it. Home is a place that you are glad to drive into at night, eager to open the front door.

A joyful atmosphere is encouraged when parents are sensitive to the ever-changing needs of the family. Just as the gardener is alert to and anticipating the different needs of his plants, we must recognize and anticipate the needs of our children.

Is a preteen being bombarded with hormonal changes? Perhaps a reassuring reminder about what's happening will bring comfort, especially when the parent recalls her own experience of this time in life. What's needed here is a kind voice that says "I understand. And even though everything seems hard now, this too will pass." A new piece of clothing or a new hairdo is a great "pick-me-up" for an emerging teenage girl. Simply rearranging a bedroom will give an emotional boost in the awkward season of change. Some "space" may also be appreciated. Gently alerting siblings "to leave her alone" can alleviate potential disagreements.

Is a young child anxious about a new school? An alert parent will notice the emotions of his child and provide comfort and encouragement. A special outing with Dad in celebration of this new school year provides an opportunity to discuss what's coming up.

Perhaps a nervous five-year-old simply needs to know that his dad was once nervous, too, but that his dad has confidence in him.

A gift that we can give to our children is perspective. There's a good chance that we have experienced many of the things our children will face. But we also need the perspective of the gardener. He knows that his job is never finished. Next season will bring new challenges and different blessings. His garden never reaches perfection. There are always changes, always needs. His joy is in the process itself.

We will never "arrive" in family life. When I was surrounded with small children, I thought, *If I can just hang on until they are older, I can relax.* It was as if I viewed life as a ladder rather than a garden. I was always struggling to get to the next rung, the next season in life. So focused would I become on simply making it to the next age that I often missed out on the blessings of the moment. And at the next age, more challenges were waiting. There were different character traits to work on and new circumstances in my own life that revealed weaknesses. Would I ever "get to the top"?

Life is not a ladder to climb to the top but a garden to enjoy. The gardener's joy is in his work, a job that is never finished. He delights in the process of the work. Our work in families is never finished. We will never perfect character, nor will our children. We are people in process. Yet there is joy in the process if we relax, knowing that the blessing is in the journey rather than in the completion of the job. When we relax, the atmosphere of our homes will become less tense and more joyful and we will rely more on the power of the Master Gardener.

THE MASTER GARDENER

The old gardener crinkles his nose as he bends over to smell the soft pink peonies. A wonderful sweet fragrance seems to surround him, and he wishes he could bottle it up and take it home. Surely no man-made perfume can match this heavenly scent.

Straightening his bent frame, he glances toward heaven ever mindful that he is but a tool in the Master's hand. He knows that God creates the seasons. He designs the plants—each one so different and yet so perfect. His is a God of detail and He makes no mistakes. Knowing the needs of His creation, God brings the rains and the sun to provide nurture. Often God's ways and His timing seem curious to the gardener, but he knows that what God does is best. The gardener simply delights in the fact that he has been chosen to discover, to enjoy, and to make beautiful what God has already created.

How often I seem to forget that God is the Master Gardener in my home. Too frequently I attempt to take His job. After all, there are so many good books on parenting today. Plus, I come from a strong Christian family myself, and I married into one as well. I've listened to numerous tapes and speakers on the family. Surely I should have this down pat by now.

And then I fail once again. I lash out at a child who was not at fault. I say something to my husband I shouldn't. I totally flunk the test of compassion. I feel sorry for myself because a friend let me down. And then I feel guilty because I should know better. So I determine to try harder. And I fail again. And finally I go to God and say, "I can't do it." And He cheers!

God knows I can't become the person I desire to be or raise my kids with the character He wants. Only He can do it. My frustration comes because I want to be God. It all goes back to the first garden, Eden. Adam and Eve got themselves into trouble because they, too, wanted to be equal with God. They wanted all knowledge and power. And I want that same power—the power that will ensure that I raise the ideal family. Frustration comes because I don't have the perfect formula nor the power to make it happen. Only God does.

God's grace, not perfect formulas or competent parents, will build character in the lives of our families. My own failures will cause me either to become frustrated or to become dependent. Frustration says, "I should be able to do it." Whereas dependence says, "I can't. God, please, You do it in Your way in Your time in me and in my kids." God's power is perfected in our weaknesses (2 Corinthians 12:9). That's why He cheers when I come to the end of my resources and turn back to His.

The lovely fragrances permeate the entire garden, the natural result of the Master Gardener's work. An unseen presence reflects the beauty; the old gardener can't produce the fragrance. He can merely cultivate a garden to produce it. Yet as the fragrance spreads, others are drawn by its loveliness to view the beautiful garden.

In a similar manner, when we fall back on the Master Gardener, His love will be a fragrance in our families, and others will be drawn to Him. "But thanks be to God, who always leads us in triumphal procession in Christ and through us spreads everywhere the fragrance of the knowledge of him. For we are to God the aroma of Christ" (2 Corinthians 2:14–15, NIV).

Integrity, a teachable spirit, self-discipline, compassion, a servant's heart, courage, faith, and joy—these are the fundamental characteristics of moral character. We can only cultivate the home, seek to plant the seeds, and care for the plants. The development is up to God.

Dear Lord,

No human advice or wisdom or gallant efforts will be able to bring about the character in my family that You desire and that I want. Only You, O Lord, can do that. Once again I relinquish myself and my family into Your hands. Make us what You have created us to be. And help us to be a reflection of Your faithfulness. Amen

FOCUS QUESTIONS

Meditate on Psalm 46

1. What are the attributes of our heavenly Father contained in this psalm?

2. In what ways are you trying to be the "perfect parent" and failing?

3. What would God say to you if He were right here to put His loving arms around you at this very moment?

4. Have a time of thanking God that you are His, your children are His, and your mate is His. He alone is able to be the Master Gardener.

5. Write your own psalm of thanksgiving to God for what He has done in your life.

Meditate on Ephesians 3:20–21, memorizing this as a promise for your family.

For nothing will be impossible with God.
(Luke 1:37)

APPENDIX ONE:
OUR FAVORITE BOOKS

*H*ere is a list of our favorite books. We have asked each of our children to read the first list by high school graduation and the second by college graduation.

These books are in no particular order of importance. Our desire has been for *variety*. You may have others to add, or you may enjoy making your own family list.

There are many biographies on the high school list. We have starred the easiest ones to read. Our goal is to get our kids reading and to expose them to a sampling of the good books available which will encourage their faith.

One reference book to mention is *A Ready Defense* by Josh McDowell (Here's Life Pub.). Every family should have this book, and the kids should be familiar with its contents so that they will know how to use it as needed.

TEN CLASSICS OF THE FAITH FOR HIGH SCHOOL STUDENTS

1. *Power Through Prayer,* E. M. Bounds (Springdale, PA: Whitaker House, 1982).

2. **God's Smuggler,* Brother Andrew (Old Tappan, NJ: NAL, 1967).

3. **The Hiding Place,* Corrie Ten Boom (Old Tappan, NJ: Revell, 1971).

4. *Three Steps Forward, Two Steps Back,* Chuck Swindoll (New York City, NY: Bantam, 1980).

5. *Through Gates of Splendor*, Elizabeth Elliot (Wheaton, IL: Tyndale, 1986), or *Blood Brothers*, Elias Chacour and David Hazard (Grand Rapids, MI: Chosen Books, 1984).

6. *Love, Sex and the Whole Person*, Tim Stafford (Grand Rapids, MI: Campus Life-Zondervan, 1991).

7. *Pursuit of Holiness*, Jerry Bridges (Colorado Springs, CO: NavPress, 1978).

8. *The Fight*, John White (Downer's Grove, IL: Intervarsity Press, 1976).

9. *Bruchko*, Bruce Olson,(Altamonte Springs, FL: Creation House, 1973)

10. *This Present Darkness*, Frank E. Peretti (Wheaton, IL: Crossway Books, 1986).

* denotes easy readers

TEN CLASSICS OF THE FAITH FOR COLLEGE STUDENTS

1. *Mere Christianity*, C. S. Lewis (New York City, NY: Macmillan, 1943).

2. *Born Again*, C. Colson (Tarrytown, NY: Revell, 1976).

3. *Abide in Christ*, Andrew Murray (Springdale, PA: Whitaker House, 1979).

4. *Pontius Pilate*, Paul Maier (Wheaton, IL: Living Books-Tyndale Press, 1981).

5. *Know Why You Believe*, Paul Little (Wheaton, IL: InterVarsity Press, 1988) or *Know What You Believe*, Paul Little (Wheaton, IL: Victor, 1985).

6. *The Master Plan of Evangelism*, Robert Coleman (Tarrytown, NY: Revell, 1963) or *Out of the Saltshaker*, Becky Pippert (Downer's Grove, IL: Intervarsity Press, 1979).

7. **Two from Galilee,* Marjorie Holmes (New York, NY: Bantam, 1982).

8. *Fit to Be Tied,* Bill and Lynne Hybels (Grand Rapids, MI: Zondervan, 1991).

9. *Hind's Feet on High Places,* Hannah Hurnard (Wheaton, IL: Tyndale, 1986) or *Disappointment with God,* Philip Yancey (New York City, NY: Harper Paperbacks, 1988).

10. *Basic Christianity,* John Stott (Downer's Grove, IL: Intervarsity Press, 1971) or *The Message of the Sermon on the Mount,* John Stott (Downer's Grove, IL: Intervarsity Press, 1988).

*denotes easy readers

BEST BIBLES

1. NIV Study Bible (Grand Rapids, MI: Zondervan)

2. Disciples Study Bible (Nashville, TN: Holman)

3. Harper Study Bible (Grand Rapids, MI: Zondervan).

4. The Student Bible (Grand Rapids, MI: Zondervan)

5. Life Application Bible (Wheaton, IL: Tyndale).

There are numerous good "quiet time" booklets for your children on the market today. Take them on a visit to your local Christian bookstore and help them pick one out to use. *My Utmost for His Highest* by Oswald Chambers (Zondervan) is a classic for collegians and adults.

APPENDIX TWO: DISCERNING GOD'S WILL

TEN CONCISE QUESTIONS TO ASK MYSELF WHEN SEEKING TO DISCERN GOD'S WILL

1. **Am I in a Right Relationship with God?**

   If there is unconfessed sin in my life, it is a barrier between me and God. Our fellowship is broken. See Psalms 32:1–6; 66:18–209.

2. **Do I Want to Know and Do God's Will?**

   Jesus said that whoever is *willing* to do what God wants will know (John 7:17).

3. **Have I Asked God for Wisdom? (James 1:5)**

   God promises us sound judgment (2 Timothy 1:7), but we must ask and keep on asking.

4. **Does the Bible Speak to This Decision in Any Way?**

   Some decisions have been clearly addressed in Scripture. God does not lead contrary to what He has already said in His Word.

5. **Have I Assembled and Studied All the Facts?**

   It is wise to list the pros and cons and ask, "What obligations do I already have that I must keep?"

6. **Do I Have Deep Inner Conviction and Peace About This? (Philippians 4:6–7)**

   Do I have peace and conviction about what is right? Paul says, "Anything which does not arise from conviction is sin" (Romans 14:23, NEB).

   Sometimes we must pray and fast regularly about a question before we receive God's peace. God's peace is deeper than the acceptance given by a casual world.

7. Have I Sought the Advice of Mature Christians Who Know Me Well?

Others will not always be right, but if three or four mature Christians agree, their opinions must be seriously considered. Always ask others to *pray* for you as well as advise you.

8. Will This Help Me to Better Love God and My Neighbor?

This is the most important goal in life. If something hinders this goal, we must carefully examine the problem (Matthew 22:37–39).

9. Is This My Decision to Make?

I may be worrying about something that will eventually be decided by someone else.

10. Do I Have to Decide Now, or Can It Wait?

Often we worry needlessly about decisions that are not really pressing. Sometimes they go away.

ONE FINAL THOUGHT

When we ask for guidance, often God will not answer immediately for He knows we are not yet ready for that knowledge.

Some of us are struggling and striving to know God's will when we ought to be simply seeking to get to know God. (Psalm 46:10: "Cease striving and know that I am God.") Paul said, "Everything else is worthless when compared with the priceless gain of knowing Christ Jesus my Lord. All I care for is to know Christ" (Philippians 3:7–10, NEB).

There is a very subtle danger here for persons who are struggling to know God's will. You don't have to struggle to know God's will; you simply have to back up and get to know God better. Then you will understand when He speaks to you.

APPENDIX THREE:
LEADER'S GUIDE FOR A GROUP STUDY

INTRODUCTION TO LEADING A SMALL GROUP

One of the best ways to use this book is to pull together a few others, agree to meet regularly, and discuss how these chapters apply to you in your individual lives and in your family. You do not need to be an experienced leader to start such a group. After all, the Lord has promised to be with us when we gather in His name. Once people begin to interact with this book and with one another, God has a way of helping us learn from one another and grow in wonderful ways.

The goal of such a group is simply to encourage each other in the challenges of family life. The discussion questions we have provided below will help you get going, but you will often find that the discussions that follow after the questions produce the greatest benefit.

There are numerous simple booklets available at your local Christian bookstore on how to lead a successful small group, and we encourage you to study one if you feel the need. (A good one: James Nyquist and Jack Kurhatschek, *Leading Bible Discussions,* Downer's Grove, IL, Intervarsity Press).

1. *Pray* for the right people to join the group and then approach those whom you feel best about inviting. Twelve to fourteen people is about as many as you will be able to effectively involve. Agree on the time, place, frequency of meetings, and length of meetings suitable to the group. We strongly urge you to include some single parents.

2. No two groups are alike. Some will have experienced believers familiar with Scripture and with the concepts in this book. Oth-

ers will be new seekers. Some will jell easily with members willing to share personally; others will need time to speak out and share personally. In some groups, prayer will be natural; in others it may be awkward at first.

3. Be sensitive to the needs of the group. Make each person feel important and comfortable. Be gentle and loving. Be flexible. Most importantly, pray for your group members daily throughout the study. Be in touch with them by phone. A leader's role is one of *encouragement*.

4. As the leader, you will set the pattern for the others in your openness, your honesty, your acceptance of other viewpoints, and in your flexibility. Use the suggested questions as enablers to help the group talk openly about their response to the book, but don't be bound by these questions. You will often come up with other questions and ideas that will be even more suitable for your group.

5. Your group will gain much more in their discussions if the individuals have taken the time prior to the meetings not just to have read the assigned chapter in advance, but also to have privately recorded their own responses to the Focus Questions at the end of each chapter.

6. If you are leading a group experienced in Bible study and desire a more demanding challenge, we recommend that you take the biblical characters of either Nehemiah or Daniel and study how each man exhibited the character traits described in each chapter.

Have a wonderful time and may God richly bless your group!

DISCUSSION QUESTIONS: INTRODUCTORY SESSION

1. Have a time of introductions. Each person might share along the lines of where they were born, hobbies, children and ages, spouse, etc.

2. Ask the question, "Who in your life is a personal hero (or three heroes if the group is small) or positive role model, and why?"

(The person can be dead or alive.) Share the traits you most admire in the person. Appoint a secretary to list all of the character traits mentioned. After everyone has shared, review the list of traits that the group mentioned. What traits were most often mentioned? Why?

3. Give a brief description of the book. Ask them to read chapter 1 and complete the Focus Questions before the next meeting.

4. Have each person share what he or she hopes to get from the study. Then close in prayer. You might have each person pray for the person on his or her right, remembering what they hoped to get out of the study.

SESSION FOLLOWING CHAPTER 1: THE CRISIS OF CHARACTER

Open in Prayer

1. Have several in the group share about a personal experience that had a major impact on their view of success—success in community, career success, success as a Christian, success in marriage. Have they tried to discuss this experience with their children? What were the results?

2. In the chapter, we read of a mother whose child needed to be kept home even though the child wanted to go play with her friend. Do any of you identify with this dilemma of having to say no when your child is pressuring you. How have you handled these experiences? What were the results? What was your long-range goal?

3. Have someone summarize the *expedient* type of character. Can anyone identify with this type of personality? Does anyone have a child at this stage? Give an example of your behavior or your child's behavior. How can we ourselves move beyond this behavior? How can we help our children to grow as well?

4. Discuss in the same way, the *malleable* character and the *legalistic character.*

5. Perhaps some parent would like to discuss a current challenge they are having with a child and ask advice. Or perhaps someone has gained a helpful insight this week in regard to improving communication in the home and would like to share it.

6. Before you close the meeting, spend some time in prayer, asking God's help on situations shared in the group tonight.

For additional study: the book of Jonah

SESSION FOLLOWING CHAPTER 2: INTEGRITY

Open in Prayer

1. Can someone share a memory from childhood that etched in his or her mind the importance of integrity? How has that made a difference in this person's life?

2. Does someone remember an occasion when one parent openly acknowledged a failure or a mistake? What impression did it make?

3. Which of the four ingredients that need to be "built into" a person of integrity did you most respond to and why?

4. In what area of your life do you have the greatest difficulty maintaining consistency? What practical steps might help you grow in this area?

5. Describe a challenge a family member faced that provided an opportunity for growth in honesty.

6. Most young children will lie. What do you think is most effective in teaching children to speak the truth?

7. What were the two things that need to be "cleaned out" of our lives if we want to become people of integrity? Can you think of others?

8. How has a failure helped you or one of your children grow in integrity?

9. Divide into prayer partners; share an area in your life or the life of one of your children that relates to integrity. Take a few minutes to pray for each other.

For additional study: Proverbs 3:1–7

SESSION FOLLOWING CHAPTER 3: TEACHABLE SPIRIT

Open in Prayer

1. Do you know someone who has a teachable spirit? How is this expressed or communicated?

2. Review the four components of a teachable spirit. Which one "hit home" as you thought about your own family? Why?

3. What are some specific ways to demonstrate to others that you value them?

4. In considering discernment, what are our priorities in decision making?

5. How can we help our children develop discernment?

6. Describe someone who has given you a fresh perspective at a time when you needed it. Is there a step you can take to broaden your perspective?

7. What are you doing to grow spiritually? To grow in other ways?

8. Share a blessing that you have learned from a difficult experience.

9. What action do you plan to take in order to develop a teachable spirit within your family?

10. Spend some time as a group thanking God for specific things you have learned from one another.

For additional study: Proverbs 15:31–33

SESSION FOLLOWING CHAPTER 4:
SELF-DISCIPLINE

Open in Prayer

1. What recent national events demonstrate the need for self-discipline? What have been the results of lack of self-discipline for the nation or for the people involved?

2. Can someone share some mistakes or some wise actions of their parents in teaching self-discipline?

3. Tell of some difficult experiences that, in the long run, you realize taught you self-discipline or patience.

4. Of the seven principles given in this chapter, which one seems most applicable to your family at this time? Why?

5. Do you and your mate have a unified approach to discipline? What have you done to develop and maintain unity?

6. Share something that you as a parent have done to help your child grow in responsibility.

7. Is one of your children going through a difficult time at the moment? How might this difficulty be used to build endurance?

8. Divide into twos or threes and ask the group to share an area in their own life or in the life of their child in which greater self-discipline is needed. Take turns praying for one another.

For additional study: James 3:2–10, Proverbs 29:15–17

SESSION FOLLOWING CHAPTER 5:
COMPASSION

Open in Prayer

1. Discuss the difference between sympathy and compassion. Is compassion a quality that is really appreciated and noticed among your circle of friends?

2. Have you hesitated to get involved recently in some situation where your help was needed? Why did you hesitate? Do you think you should have acted differently? What do the others think?

3. Could someone tell of a time in which he or she experienced a whole new deeper awareness of the compassion of God?

4. Share about a time when the idea "it could be me" or "it could be Christ" was personally helpful in causing you to be more patient, understanding, or helpful to another.

5. Describe some situation that might arise within the home when compassion is appropriate and one in which it is not appropriate.

6. How can we encourage greater compassion among family members toward one another?

7. What is one way that this chapter has spoken to you?

8. Spend some time praying together for personal needs within the group.

For additional study: Matthew 25:31–46

SESSION FOLLOWING CHAPTER 6: SERVANT'S HEART

Open in Prayer

1. What do you find to be your most difficult challenge in serving others?

2. Share an experience when you cared for someone else even though you did not feel like it.

3. Describe someone that you know who is naturally thoughtful. How has this thoughtfulness been expressed?

4. What manners are important to you? How are you training your children in manners?

5. We read of four areas in which to be generous: time, possessions, talents, and relationships. In which area have you taken
some positive steps with your children? How has this happened?

6. What has helped you learn to appreciate others? How can you
help your children with this?

7. Prayer is one of the greatest ways we can serve others, yet often
it is the most difficult. Why is this so? How can we more effectively pray for others?

8. With so many needs around us, how can we determine what we
should do? How can we provide opportunities for our children
to care for others?

9. Spend some time in group prayer thanking God for the specific
ways others have served you and your family.

For additional study: Romans 12:9–21

SESSION FOLLOWING CHAPTER 7: COURAGE

Open in Prayer

1. Take turns sharing about incidents that caused you to be afraid.
Did this turn into a positive experience in which courage over-
ruled fear, or did fear have the victory? How would you handle
the situation differently today?

2. We read of three typical responses to fear: deny it, be overcome
by it, face it. Which response do you most identify with? What
is most helpful to you in facing your fears?

3. What enables you to be completely honest with God about your
fears? What Scripture passages are most encouraging? Review
Psalm 139.

4. We read of three foundational elements which help stimulate
the development of courage: personal security, clear convictions,

and a sense of destiny. How do we get personal security? What is one thing we can do this week to build our child's security?

5. What are the most important convictions to you? How can you pass these along to your children?

6. Describe what a sense of personal destiny means to you. How has this been formed?

7. Several things were mentioned that are helpful in giving our children a sense of destiny. What have you found helpful? What do you plan to do in the future to help your children in this area?

8. The source of our courage must be our heavenly Father. Spend some time remembering specific examples in the Bible in which He faithfully led fearful individuals through steps of courage.

9. Spend some time in prayer, thanking Him for steps of courage in your life and in the lives of others.

For additional study: Psalm 56, Joshua 1

SESSION FOLLOWING CHAPTER 8: FAITH

Open in Prayer

1. A vital Christian home will have a freedom to be honest about our faith, our struggles, and our victories. Can you describe some homes like this? What has helped you to create this kind of home?

2. What has made God's Word become alive to you? Share a passage in Scripture that has meant the most to you recently.

3. How are you encouraging your children to develop a love of God's Word?

4. We read about three ways in which God answers prayer: yes, no, and wait. Share an example of a no answer and a wait answer. How has your understanding of God's love grown as a result of these answers?

5. Share some ideas which you have for making prayer more vital in your family.

6. Fellowship is an important ingredient for spiritual growth. Do you have a few people to whom you are accountable? How have these relationships encouraged your growth? If you do not yet have this type of relationship with someone, how can it be developed?

7. What are you doing to encourage your children to build strong friendships with peers who are growing in Christ?

8. Do you worship together on Sundays? A church experience will become most meaningful when we give of our time and talents to this body of Christ. What are we doing as individuals and as families to serve the church?

9. Divide into small groups and spend some time in prayer for one another's spiritual growth and one another's families.

For additional study: Hebrews 3:1–4:3

SESSION FOLLOWING CHAPTER 9: JOY

Open in Prayer

1. What do you understand to be the meaning of *joy* as described in this chapter? Is it a fair, reasonable definition from your perspective? What do various people in your group think?

2. When do we most often experience true joy?

3. What are factors that rob us of joy in the family? How have you sought to deal with these "enemies" of joy?

4. Do you know of some families that seem to do a good job of maintaining a joyful spirit in the home? How do they do it?

5. What do different families do to create an attitude of gratefulness to God, helping parents and children to be more aware of God's blessings?

6. Are there certain things that have helped you keep more of an eternal perspective? What? How can we help one another get beyond fears of dying?

7. Are there things going on now in our own lives, our communities, our city, our church, or our nation that are making it difficult for us to express God's peace and joy? How might we encourage one another in these things?

8. Spend some time in prayer, first adoring God for who He is—His attributes—and second, thanking Him for what He has done—His blessings.

For additional study: Psalm 145

SESSION FOLLOWING CHAPTER 10:
THE HOME WHERE CHARACTER BLOSSOMS

Open in Prayer

1. What meant the most to you in this final chapter?

2. What are some areas that you feel you have been failing in personally or as a parent? How are you handling failure? How does God see these failures?

3. What are some specific blessings of this "season"?

4. Describe some of the different gifts of your mate, your children. How can these differences have a positive influence on your family?

5. Is your tendency to see life as a "ladder" or as a "garden"? How can you maintain a balance between doing your part in the family and yet believing (and living as if) God is the true Head of the family?

6. In reflecting on the study of this whole book, what has been most helpful to you and why?

7. What decisions have you made as a result of this study? What actions have you taken?

8. Spend some time in prayer as a group, thanking God for the different blessings He has brought to you through this time together in the study.

For additional study: 1 Corinthians 1:4–9

NOTES

Chapter One: The Crisis of Character

1. Stephen R. Covey, *The Seven Habits of Highly Effective People* (New York: Simon and Schuster, 1989), 5.

2. "Pulpit Helps" (Chattanooga, TN: November 1989), 16.

3. Here's a further thought on this subject from John:

Nowhere have I seen this more clearly illustrated than in the musical *Les Misérables*. If you have never seen it, I hope that you will. The more you hum those majestic melodies and reflect on the plot, the more you realize that this musical drama is really a deep and wonderful study of character development and character type. Victor Hugo, the author of the original novel, was writing about real people and personality types of the France of one hundred fifty years ago, but people are still the same. Most of the people we know will fall into one of the four general categories described in this chapter, and each of these types is represented in *Les Misérables*.

The Expedient Character

This is represented by Thénardier, the rascally inn-keeper, the robber of corpses, and eventually the Duke de Thenardier. He is the sort of person who basically does exactly what he wants to do all the time. His own personal gratification is what matters most, and he will happily steal, murder, betray to get what he wants. He is not completely oblivious to the approval of others and he will only do what he knows he can get by with. He wants admiration and applause from others and likes nothing better than to bilk those whom he is buttering up. Expediency is his middle name.

The Malleable Character

The young girl, Cosette, is portrayed as an attractive, but rather superficial person, who does not seem to have a mind of her own. She is greatly influenced by her stepfather, by her fiancé, and by others. She is certainly not a bad person in any way, and in fact, she comes across as rather a good person. But as one contemplates upon her nature, it seems that her principles are not deeply embedded in her character. The malleable person does not think for himself or herself but rather goes along with the crowd.

The Legalistic Character

Chief Inspector Javert is portrayed as the villain, but actually is a very fine and highly principled man who has lived all of his life in obedience to the law of the

187

land. He believes deeply in right over wrong and is committed to not just living for and living by the right, but enforcing what is right in the world. He is honest, hard-working, courteous, and consistent, but there is no mercy or compassion in the man. He lives and dies by the law and cannot accept that there may be gray areas in between right and wrong or that people who have been wrong can change and become new people. The legalist will never get into trouble, but he will not be an encourager to others seeking to become better people.

The Principled Character

The great man of *Les Misérables* is Jean Valjean. The ex-convict whose life is turned around by the gracious treatment he receives at the hand of the saintly bishop. Valjean becomes not only a hard-working and successful business leader but also mayor of the community. He is committed to the right and is filled with compassion for those who have gone astray or find themselves in need. A major difference between Valjean and the legalistic Javert is that while Valjean is committed to the law he also realizes that some laws are higher than others. Notably, that mercy is above justice. He does not live by the letter of the law, but rather by the principles which the law imperfectly seeks to produce in society.

Chapter Two: Integrity

1. Mary Ann Ekman, *Why Kids Lie,* quoted in an article by Sally Squires entitled, "For Children, Lying Comes Naturally" in *The Washington Post,* Health Section (7 November 1989), 9.

Chapter Four: Self-Discipline

1. For further studies on disciplining children see:

   Susan A. Yates, *And Then I Had Kids, Encouragement for Mothers of Young Children* (Brentwood, TN: Wolgemuth & Hyatt, 1988) and John W. Yates, *For the Life of the Family* (Wilton, CT: Morehouse-Barlow Pub., 1986).

2. Two good source books are James Dobson, *Dare to Discipline* (Wheaton, IL: Tyndale, 1973) and *The Strong-Willed Child* (Wheaton, IL: Tyndale, 1978).

Chapter Five: Compassion

1. Laura Sessions Stepp, "Focus on Self Has Changed Language of Sacrifice," *The Washington Post* (24 March 1991).
2. Matthew 5:7, John's own paraphrase of the original.
3. Paul Lee Tan, *Encyclopedia of 7,700 Illustrations* (Rockville, MD: Assurance Pub., 1985), 530.
4. Ibid., 529.

Chapter Six: A Servant's Heart

1. *Webster's New World Dictionary* (Warner Books, 1984), 509.

Chapter Seven: Courage

1. Chainie Scott, as quoted in Christine Spolar's "Two Who Dared to Take the Stand," *The Washington Post* (19 April 1991).
2. *The World Book Encyclopedia*, Volume 6 (Chicago: World Book-Childcraft Int., Inc., 1979), 50.

Chapter Eight: Faith

1. *The Book of Common Prayer* (New York, NY: Church Hymnal Corp., 1977), 308.
2. Thoughts taken from John W. Yates, "Instilling Holy Ambition" in *Keeping Your Kids Christian,* ed. Marshall Shelley (Ann Arbor, MI: Servant Publications, 1990), 209.

Chapter Nine: Joy

1. W. E. Sangster, from a collection of his sermons in *Twenty Centuries of Great Preaching,* volume xi, (Waco, TX: Word Books, 1976), 342.
2. C. S. Lewis, *Screwtape Letters* (London: Collins Press, 1979), 51.
3. Paul Lee Tan, *Encyclopedia of 7,700 Illustrations* (Rockville, MD: Assurance Pub., 1985), 1456.
4. Henry Van Dyke, recorded in *The Hymnal, 1982* (New York, NY: Church Hymnal Corp., 1977), 376.

Chapter Ten: The Home Where Character Blossoms

1. Thoughts taken from Susan A. Yates, *And Then I Had Kids, Encouragement for Mothers of Young Children* (Brentwood, TN: Wolgemuth & Hyatt, 1988), 2.

SUBJECT INDEX

SCRIPTURE INDEX